Rishikesh

Meditations

Jose Miguel Jimenez

0

Special Thanks

I'd like of give special thanks my teachers at Shree Mahesh Heritage School of Meditation in Upper Tapovan, Rishikesh, India for all the knowledge they passed on to me during my time there. Ram Gupta is the Senior Instructor and shared his endless store of knowledge each day in an easy to understand manner. Yogi Dinesh Bisht was our constant motivator to remember the lessons from before and a good friend who made learning such a pleasure. Chitrangana Rawat kept us focused each afternoon with studies of Mantra meditation, while Naina Panwar created a fun atmosphere as we learned Bhajans, Prayers, and Mantras accompanied by castanets, small drums, and other musical instruments. My time there was too short and yet, I left confident in my ability to provide instruction in Meditation to those with a desire to learn. Thank you all for the incredible time spent there and for the amazing friendships I found in India. Namaste my friends.

Table of Contents

Osho Nataraj
Osho Kundalini
Pulse
Relaxation
Satnam Kirtan
Sahaj Yog Dhyan (Sahaja Yoga)
Satsang
Self Inquiry
Transcendental Meditation
Trataka (Candle)
Vipassana
Walking
Yantra
Yoga Nidra

Section IV: Pictorial Guide & Additional Information
Glossary
Overview of Practices
Meditation Chants
The Eight Limbs of Yoga
The Wonders of 5 (Pancha) Overview
Structure of the Yoga Sutra
Seven Chakra Meditation Structure
The Bhagavad Gita Saar
Marma (Energy Points)
Kundalini Energy Illustration
Typical Meditation Session Structure outline
Sample Meditation Sessions

Preface

The term Meditation carries with it a sense of the unknown and is often misunderstood by Westerners unfamiliar with a centuries old practice originating in Eastern countries. Like many others before me, I had only the barest of knowledge associated with Meditation stemming from my minimum exposure coming from vague references in literature, movies, and television. Joan Matlock, a close friend, heard I was traveling to New Zealand and suggested I look into a Vipassna Meditation course offered at the Dhamma Medini Meditation Center located just outside of Auckland, New Zealand.

After investigating the conditions for attending, I requested to be included in a ten-day silent meditation course to be held a few months away when I would be traveling across the country. Eleven days of complete silence with no connection to the outside world left me a changed man and the hunger for further exposure became a growing need within my psyche. My next step was to find a suitable school to attend, and thanks once again to my friend Joan, I traveled to Rishikesh, India to be part of the Shree Mahesh Heritage Meditation School 300-hour Instructor course. For one month I breathed, meditated, studied, and lived Meditation within walking distance of the Ganges; holiest of rivers found in India.

I'd like to believe that like many Americans when I heard the term Yoga, I always believed it to be one of those classes with someone at the front of the room directing me into a twisting position which usually left me with stretched out muscles and a certain sense of physical exertion. I never made the connection with the two words Yoga and Meditation and always believed them to be two separate and different practices, when in reality they are one.

Yoga Meditation has its origins approximately 3000 years ago in Northern India. Today, Yoga can be found in all parts of the globe, but Rishikesh, India is widely considered to be the home of Yoga and instruction can be found there among its many schools, or Ashramas. My journey took me to this city situated near the banks of the Ganges river whose holy waters beckon to travelers and religious pilgrims alike.

In order to further my personal store of knowledge concerning Yoga, I have been reading about Swami Vivekananda, one of the best known proponents of Yoga who gained significant notoriety as he traveled first India, then later the globe extolling its virtues. Vijay Goel, author of *Complete Book of Yoga* has collected Vivekananda's manuscripts covering: Karma Yoga, Bhakti Yoga, Raja Yoga, and Jnana Yoga.

Another text I will be referring to is *The Bhagavad Gita* translated by Eknath Easwaran from the original Sanskrit. The text is a 700 verse scripture that is part of the Hindu epic Mahabharata and consists of conversations between the warrior "Arjuna" and his spiritual guide "Sri Krishna" as they discuss the questions often presented through one's lifetime. The Gita upholds the essence and the theological tradition of the Veda and Upnishads. It is considered by Eastern and Western scholars to be among the greatest spiritual books the world has known. In terms of pure spiritual knowledge, the Bhagavad Gita is incomparable. Its intrinsic beauty is how its knowledge applies to all humans and does not postulate any sectarian ideology, or secular view. The text reveals the eternal principles which are fundamental and essential for spiritual life from all perspectives and allows one to perfectly understand the esoteric truths hidden within all religious scriptures. This is accomplished in a clear and wonderful way where the supreme Lord Krishna describes the science of self-realization with incredible examples.

Also, a third reference text is *Hatha Yoga Pradipika* by Pancham Sinh. For the purposes of this text I will give some insight into first Hatha Yoga and then Raja Yoga as these were the two primary systems I received instruction in. Finally, I am incorporating much of the content provided me by Shree Mahesh Heritage Meditation School during my attendance there.

There, my fellow classmates and I, began our studies early in the morning, and ended our practice in the early evening. On weekends, we traveled to different locations high in the Himalayas to meditate at various temples, religious caves, and listened to holy men whose power over their physical selves allowed them to withstand great extremes in temperature. To say the experience was difficult and challenging would be an understatement, but the rewards were completely worth the long hours spent in various meditation poses, accompanied by chants, prayers, songs, and laughter.

Once more, another hunger was recognized and I knew deep within the consciousness of me I had a need to return home and share the abundant knowledge given to me by Ram Kumar Gupta, lead Instructor and his amazing staff. As a retired English Professor I understand the need for a concise textbook required when teaching and am familiar with how such an informative guide could be created. I decided to take the information I had been given during my tenure at Shree Mahesh Heritage Meditation School and construct this instructional manual to support my own teaching of Meditation.

Also, I believe a comprehensive guide can help to clear the fog of misunderstanding many may have when it comes to Meditation by providing a manual for those who don't have the resources, or the time to travel to India as I did. Within the pages that follow, readers can discover the roots of Meditation and how connecting to such an ancient practice can give their lives meaning, while finding joy and acceptance of the place they find themselves each and every day.

I'd like to add that much of the text that follows may at times, seem unsupported by research, but in my own defense I have been using information provided to me by my teachers who like many before, have passed on knowledge gained from intensive study and word of mouth. When necessary to add clarity, I have relied heavily on Yogapedia and other sources I was able to locate through searches on the internet and available texts. I believe in the substance of this manual and offer it as a guide, and not an authoritative script heavily supported by exact references, much as it was offered to me. Please accept what you will and when in doubt, do as I did, and complete your own search for clarification.

Finally, by offering this comprehensive guide, my sincerest wishes are that anyone can find their own path to Meditation. Namaste my dear readers and if you ever find you have any questions about Meditation, please feel free to look me up on Instagram at (travels_withmike) or Facebook (Mike Jimenez) and YouTube (theitinerantmonk)

Section I (Theory)
Chapter I

Introduction to Meditation

What is Meditation:

Meditation can be described as an art of seeing without the interference of one's conditioned mind. Withdraw your attention from all of the objects, situations, relationships, and look within yourself. This is Meditation.

Meditation is an un-interrupted flow of self-consciousness towards the absolute existence/supreme consciousness.

Meditation is a process to know who we really are and implies turning your attention from what is finite and transient and directing it to the Divine; the eternal and absolute Existence/Consciousness.

Meditation is all about being conscious and aware of our actions, thoughts, and feelings which can be practiced continuously regardless of our surroundings.

"Meditation is listening to the Divine within." Edgar Cayce

"Meditation is a state of no-mind. Meditation is a state of pure consciousness with no content. Ordinarily, your consciousness is too full of rubbish much like a mirror covered in dust. The mind is in a constant and never- ending traffic; day in and day out. Even when you are asleep, the mind is functioning as it dreams, thinking, filled with worries and anxieties. It is preparing for the next day all the while a sub-conscious preparation is occurring. Meditation is just the opposite. Silence results from the lack of traffic and thinking has ceased. You are utterly silent when no thoughts move and desires do not stir." Osho

"Meditation is like giving a hug to ourselves as we get in touch with the awesome reality in us. While in Meditation we feel a deep sense of intimacy with God and a love that is inexplicable." Paramhansa Yogananda

In the light of the above definitions of Meditation we can say, "Meditation is the art and science of systematically observing, accepting, understanding, and training each of the levels of our being such that we may coordinate and integrate those aspects of ourselves as we dwell in the direct experience of the center of consciousness.

What is *Not* Meditation

Before we know anything about Meditation, it is important to familiarize ourselves with all those practices and beliefs which are often considered as Meditation, but most definitely **aren't** Meditation.

Meditation is not Concentration: In the initial phase of learning Meditation, concentration is a useful tool to aid the student, but should not be considered the essence of Meditation. Instead, Meditation is awareness of the moment without choosing anything to concentrate upon whereas total concentration is about focusing all of your attention towards a particular task or activity. Do not confuse the two as they are completely different.

Meditation is not Relaxation: It is a by product; a natural outcome of Meditation is relaxation.

Meditation is not a religious practice: Meditation is not a specific ritual demanding sitting in a particular posture, chanting some specific Mantra, or burning incense. Also, it is not performing a particular exercise in a certain pose. Meditation is a quality of our existence. When you are aware of your *true self* and perform anything with awareness, then it becomes Meditation.

Meditation is not a state of mind: It is a state of no mind: There are many products available in today's society which promise to take us into a meditative state (alpha) of mind. Scientists have observed there are four basic states of mind depending upon the frequency of mind waves: alpha, beta, gamma, and theta. Beta is the state in which we live and perform all of our day-to-day activities. Alpha is the state just below Beta. This Alpha state is often known as the state of Meditation. Gamma and Theta are the other states of mind. However, the Alpha state is not Meditation. Meditation is the awareness of our true self while in the Alpha state. You will be in Meditation if you remain awake and aware of the present moment while experiencing absolute calm. There are no trick gadgets, or devices to create awareness and instead provide conditions to aid the practitioner to realize what is "true awareness."

Meditation is not self-hypnosis: In both self-hypnosis and in many techniques of meditation at least an initial period of concentration on an object is required. But, in Meditation, the Meditator maintains an awareness of the moment, remaining conscious of the meditative process which is not exactly the case in hypnosis. In the hypnotic trance there is a lack of awareness while in the semi-conscious trance.

Meditation is not thinking: Instead, it is the process of transcending the thought process. The mind is a constant chatterbox which continues to create all sorts of good/bad, relevant/irrelevant thoughts incessantly. In Meditation we realize that we are not just the body and mind. There exists in each of us an awareness independent of all kinds of thought. Discovering this awareness is what Meditation is all abcut.

Meditation Do's and Don'ts:

Choose a time that works for you. Make an appointment with yourself and practice at the same time each day. Just as you feed your physical body several times a day at certain times, Meditation nourishes your inner life so set at least one special time each day for your Meditation exercises. The ancient teachers say that the ideal time is just around sunrise (Brahm Muhurt) and sunset (Sandhya) are particularly nice for Meditation. An excellent time to meditate is in the morning before you enter into your daily activities. However, if this is not convenient, choose another time which works better. Meditate before meals and just before going to bed. This will help you to sleep soundly.

Not on your bed. Meditating on your bed can create confusion in the unconscious mind resulting in the association with sleep when performing Meditation

How long and how often? It is very useful to make a decision on this point. The ideal duration of a Meditation sitting must be equivalent to your age. Then, allow yourself the flexibility of breaking the duration into two, or three more sections for your practice.

If you miss your scheduled Meditation: Be sure to include a session later in the day.

When you're too tired at the end of the day: It would be better for that you train yourself to sit for one minute, or a count of 10 breaths. The act of sitting for just that moment will affirm your intent to be inward for Meditation and will have a positive effect on development of good habit

Use the same place: Using the same place for Meditation each day will make a connection to the special place for your quiet, joy filled inner journey.

Choose a place where you will not be disturbed. Be certain you are out of the flow of traffic in your home so as not to be disturbed by others.

Purpose: Choose a location which is not used for any other purpose. The room should be one that is quiet and set aside for the purpose of Meditation only.

Quiet – Pleasant – Comfortable: Your space should be quiet, pleasant, and comfortable and not overly stimulating to the senses. A Meditator knows it is not sound which disturbs the Meditation you are performing, but instead it is our reaction to that sound. Absolute stillness is not necessary, but there should be a minimum of distractions.

When should we Meditate?

Ideally you should meditate every day at the same time.

The recommended time for your Meditation is 10-20 minutes once or twice each day.

Meditate on an empty stomach, or at least two hours after eating a big meal. (It is okay to meditate if you have eaten a piece of fruit)

Maintain a good posture with the back straight, long neck, and chin parallel to the floor.

The best time of day is in the morning after rising (before eating) and in the evening just before dinner. Some people may meditate at noon before lunch.

Meditation is best practiced before sleep as it can convert whole sleep into a meditative sleep which will improve the quality of sleep and enhance the self-healing process.

Meditate prior to aerobic exercise.

It is okay to meditate after a gentle Yoga practice. For any strenuous Yoga practice, please meditate before.

Benefits and Goals of Meditation:

Meditation is your personal experiment performed in the laboratory of your own mind and body. Your practice will be inspired by teachers and guided by the practices. Yet, in the end the form your practice takes is uniquely yours. Traditionally, the classical Yoga texts describe ways to attain true states of Meditation. Following these pasic techniques help you to set up the discipline of regular sitting and teach you how to get your body comfortable, find inner focus, and keep your mind from running rampant.

A successful Meditation practice requires balancing polarities, focusing and letting go, providing structure, and freedom. However, there is a need to work with guidelines for posture, concentration, breath awareness, and self-inquiry. There is also the need to understand when it is time to let go of the rules and follow the signals coming from your own consciousness. This requires openness, creativity, and discernment.

The spiritual benefit of Meditation, if done on a regular basis, is supreme bliss or enlightenment. Additional benefits practitioners can find are:
o A positive attitude towards life
o A healthy way to handle stress
o Increased clarity and improved decision making
o Increased concentration, creativity, and spontaneity
o A better understanding and control of the mind and body
o Increased inner ability to solve complex problems
  o More emotional and mental stability accompanied by a deep sense of peace and relaxation
  o Reduced bouts of anxiety and depression
  o Increased self-awareness, self-compassion, and self-confidence
  o The ability to change your reactionary habits by becoming more responsive and positive
  o Relief from chronic conditions such as pain, allergies, arthritis, indigestion, and insomnia
  o Enhanced immune system with an increased activity of natural-killer cells which aid in destroying bacteria and cancer cells
  o Increased DHEA (youth hormone) and reduced cortisol (stress hormone)
  o Healthier relationships with yourself, others, work, and life in general
  o Helps on focusing on the present moment and stop worrying about the future or past.
  o Helps to accept the things as they are and not as we desire them to be
  o Aids in lowering heart rate, normalizing blood pressure through reduced breathing, which reduces the amount of oxygen required.

Signposts of Progress in Meditation:

While the goal of Meditation is the same for everyone, the journey towards the goal is not always the same. Each person has to proceed in their own way according to the individual's capacity and mental processes available to them. Success on the path of Meditation depends not on anything exotic, but on the aspirant's undaunted will and determined effort. Journeying toward the goal is like climbing a narrow winding mountain path. As the person, climbs they encounter the same obstacles in a finer and subtler form at each stage of their journey. Meditation, according to both Yoga and Vendanta is concentration upon a single object. When concentration becomes spontaneous, it takes the form of Meditation which eventually culminates in Samadhi or total absorption. But, the state of Samadhi is not attained all at once. It is preceded by several successive stages of partial absorption. According to the scriptures of Yoga, Vedanta, and Tantra there are certain specific signs by which progress in Meditation can be ascertained. These signs include the following:

o   Mystical experiences
o   Quickness in performance
o   Degree of detachment
o   Stages of concentration
o   Depths of absorption
o   Experience of Kumbhaka, or suspension of breath
o   Depths of dispassion
o   Stages of realization
o   Experience of spiritual emotions
o   Psychic powers and attainments
o   People notice you are changing; relaxed, less reactive, more friendly
o   Increased body awareness
o   Notice a gap between stimulus & response
o   Increased calmness during and after Meditation
o   Meaningful dreams you can learn from
o   Awareness of behavior needing change
o   Passage of time during meditation speeds up

Meditation: How and What (Mechanism of Meditation)

There are two elements to any Meditation technique. These are how you pay attention and what you pay attention to. The How is usually a gentle focus which is restful and steady attention and not a harsh, or militant concentration. Also, simple acts like the sensation of breath, thoughts, or a sound created or heard. A specific focus can be used in Meditation to help interrupt the constant flow of thought. When this interruption occurs the mind naturally settles down creating a lessening flow until it appears a powerful and nourishing silence has replaced this onslaught of thoughts. A quiet mind is a natural occurrence which becomes easier to attain with a daily practice of Meditation.

Here are just a few of the many different forms of Meditation:
- o   Repeating a mantra or word out loud or silently (Transcendental, Relaxation Response, Japa)
- o   Counting or following the breath (Mindfulness, Zazen, Vipassana)
- o   Gazing at a candle flame (Trataka)
- o   Gazing at a mandala or picture of a spiritual teacher or saint (Contemplation)
- o   Feeling Compassion Meditation (Metta, Loving Kindness)
- o   Contemplative prayer/Gratitude Meditations
- o   Becoming aware of the Energy centers (Kundalini or Chakra)
- o   Meditations on various scenes or scenarios in the mind (Guided Visualizations)
- o   Meditation in motion (Yoga, Tai Chi, Walking, Sufi Dancing)

Whichever type of Meditation you choose if done correctly, will allow your body to reach a naturally occurring rest state. According to research this state is different from sleep. The rest is much deeper and at the same time is more alert. This is often called the state of restful alertness. There are many to choose from, but the most important part is to find one you like and just do it.

Chapter 2:

Nutrition and Meditation

Mitahara:

Mitahara literally means the habit of moderate intake of food and is a concept in Indian philosophy that integrates awareness about food, drink, a balanced diet, and consumption with the resulting effects on body and mind. Hatha Yoga Pradipika suggests that taste cravings should not drive one's eating habits, but recommends eat only when *one feels hungry and neither overeat, nor eat to completely fill the capacity of one's stomach. Instead, leave a quarter portion empty and fill three quarters with quality food and fresh water.* For most people, control over the diet is one of the hardest exercises because not only do we eat to satisfy our bodily needs and provide the right nutrition for system to function properly, be we tend to eat as a response to our emotional states. This not only causes us to be overweight, but frequently tires the body due to eating those foods rich in nature that do not support a healthy body as the body works harder to process the rich foods. Yoga Meditation lays down certain guidelines for a moderate diet that keeps the body strong and healthy.

The food we eat definitely has an effect on body, mind, and emotions which in turn affects our health and meditations. Whatever our individual situation and current habits, it makes a great deal of sense to personally explore the field of diet, so that we might make wise decisions. In Yoga Meditation, the desire for sustenance is one of the four primitive urges known as food, sleep, sex, and self-preservation. Wise regulation of food and the other basic drives is an important part of a foundation for Meditation.

We eat food, but not just the ingredients. When we talk of carbohydrates, proteins, fiber, vitamins, and minerals the question of diet can get quite confusing. One reason for this confusion is that we do not eat these ingredients as such. Rather, what we eat is food. If we think in terms of the foods we eat, then the whole process becomes much easier. It is not that we are not mindful of the ingredients which is quite useful, but rather we learn to think of the food itself. For example, we train ourselves to eat fresh vegetables and not just to ingest a list of nutrients which are contained in the vegetables.

What to Eat:

Vegetables:

- A mixture of green, yellow, and other seasonal vegetables provide lots of nutrition and common sense leads to a good balance of these.

Beans/Legumes:

Beans are loaded with nutrients and lots of fiber which help greatly with digestion. They are also an excellent source of protein.

Whole Grains or equivalent:

Whole grains or sprouts such as wheat, barley, rice a a great source of vitamins, minerals and fiber.

Water:

Drink a proper amount of water. This can be seen in the following: 2-3 full glasses (total of about 1 liter) at room temperature in the early morning (Ushapan) before brushing your teeth or eating. Doing so will aid in clearing out some of the toxins in your system and triggers peristalsis, the muscular movement which clears the bowels. Afterwards, food can be consumed. One sign of having enough water is the urine flows clear, unlike that found after a long sleep where no fluids were taken in.

Nutrition and cleansing:

The two functions of nutrition and cleansing work together. Each of them have two polarities. Thus, you can have food that is nutritious, or not. Likewise, you can eat foods easily digestible which facilitate cleansing and detoxifying your system, or those that aren't and block cleansing and detoxification. The questions you must ask yourself as you prepare to eat are: Does this meal provide good nutrition? Does it facilitate cleansing?

Sattvic-Rajasic-Tamasic Foods:

A diet based on Yoga and Ayurveda is strong in the Sattva Guna and leads to clarity and Upkesa (equanimity) of mind while also being beneficial to the body. Such foods include: water, cereal, grains, sprouts, legumes, fruits, milk, cheese, yoghurt, honey, peanuts, Jaggery, etc.

Foods kept overnight (leftovers) are considered Tamasic (dull, dark) as they lose their vital essences and may have grown microorganisms. Any foods that involve the harm of another being, or which harm the mind or body are also considered Tamasic. Overly sweet foods are considered Rajasic (passion/attachment). Adding too much spice, sugar, or salt may render what was a Sattvic (pure) food to become Rajasic or Tamasic. Foods considered the most Sattvic are cow's milk and fruit fallen from a tree. This is because there is absolutely no harm done to the organism from which the nutrients came, and the food was given willingly with blessings.

Scriptural References:

In Patanjali's Yoga Sutra, Tapas is found in the section on Niyama. Tapas here include Ahara Niyama, or right food in limited quantity. So, Niyama which is a personal discipline on the regulation of food habits. In other texts like Hatha Yoga Pradipika, the author insists on proper food habits. The Bhagavad Gita speaks about three types of human personality and their preference of food like Sattvic, Rajasic, and Tamasic.

Also, Buddhi (Intellect) is the aspect that knows, decides, judges, and discriminates. Often, this faculty of mind is clouded over by the habitual inner noise of attractions and aversions. One of the finest things we can do for food Sadhana (practices) is to cultivate the clarity of Buddhi by becoming ever more aware of what is useful and what is not useful. Literally ask yourself the following question: " Is this useful or not?" Your inner wisdom of Buddhi really does have a good perspective towards food, regardless of surface level actions, speech, or the thinking process. Cultivate this aspect of mind through a persistent intention by being gradual, gentle, and loving as you act on this wisdom.

Saliva (and its properties):

Usually the first act we do upon waking is to brush your teeth and rinse the mouth. For most this basic act is considered a healthy habit, but in reality it isn't. By performing this morning ritual, you are ridding yourself of the saliva and its healthy properties. A little known fact about saliva is how it reacts in the stomach to help balance the acidic nature found there. Saliva and water taken in during the day help to maintain a neutral state in the stomach. Drinking 1-2 cups of water first thing in the morning before brushing will provide the maximum potential of saliva. Water should be taken in by small sips to ensure you gain the full benefits.

Water (and food):

Today almost everyone has a habit of drinking some type of fluid as they eat such as juice, water, sodas, etc. Jatharagni (stomach fire) refers to the Ayurvedic term for a fire which aids in digestion found in the stomach and is commonly thought to be activated when we begin to eat. Drinking cold water, or other drinks can be thought to slow down, or even stop the process causing indigestion. It may be said you should never have any cold drinks before, during, or after eating due to the unhealthy nature of doing so.

However, Mattha (Buttermilk) and vegetable soup are good for your health if consumed with food. It is ideal if you consume Mattha with lunch and hot soup with dinner. Mattha is a liquid produced by constant churning of yoghurt as this produce a butter like liquid. Spices can be added to provide taste. These liquids have a water content, but their nature is not the same as water so instead of creating indigestion, they do just the opposite and aid in digesting foods.

Food and Rest:

Normally, most of us eat a meal and then begin, or resume a busy schedule of work, however this implies a lack of consideration for the food one has just consumed. In ancient times those who ate rested after meals which has become a forgotten practice in today's hectic society. Resting after a meal is good for your health and increases productivity at work and provides a refreshing break. However, this period of rest should always be taken after breakfast and lunch only. An excellent practice is to eat only two meals per day: breakfast and dinner (supper). Taking a rest time of 10-20 minutes post meal helps to create a healthy lifestyle.

One way to optimize the rest period is by lying in Vishnu Mudra on the left side on Sheshnag (reclining couch/canopy). Taking a 40 minute nap (if practical) increases your energy, but if only 10-20 minutes are all you can do, then this will be sufficient. However, the evening meal is one where you should not sleep within 2 hours of eating, but always wait for this period to expire before falling asleep.

A good practice is to sit in the Vajrasana (Thunderbolt) pose which is considered the only pose suitable after a meal. The primary function is to help in digestion of food, assists in curing knee pain, and helps the body to be stronger from the inside. A good practice is to sit in Vajrasana while watching television, or reading a book. This is an excellent posture to use after every meal, but for those whose work situation does not allow for this can wait until the evening meal. The Vajrasana pose should be performed for 5-10 minutes or more. If you are starting today, then 10 minutes may be too difficult, however after a month this should be a suitable time limit for you to achieve.

Chapter 3

Prayer and Meditation

Prayer can be considered a simple conversation with our Creator, the Universal Energy, God, or any Deity. This can be thought of as a request to meet your own needs, or those of someone else. Here we are giving thanks, or addressing a request for help to solve a situation, and possibly committing our endeavors. These prayers can be about anything and everything. Prayer provides a constant reminder of the essence of our creation and gives us a direct connection to our Creator. Prayer develops a relationship with a higher power.

It doesn't matter if you pray for yourself, or for others. Pray to heal an illness, peace in the world, or simply by sitting in silence as we quiet the mind as the effects appear to be the same. What prayer does is, at its most basic level, is to put an end to the deep-seated discomfort which all human beings experience when separated from God.

"Prayer is the place of refuge for every worry, a foundation for cheerfulness, a source of constant happiness, a protection against sadness." T. John Chrysostom

"Purity is the fruit of prayer." Blessed Mother Teresa

"We must pray without ceasing, in every occurrence and employment of our lives – that prayer which is rather a habit of lifting up the heart to God as in a constant communication with Him." Saint Elizabeth Ann Seton

"You don't know how to pray? Put yourself in the presence of God, and as soon as you have said, 'Lord, I don't know how to pray!' You can be sure you have already begun.'" St. Jose Maria Escriva

Misconceptions of Prayer:

Prayer and Meditation have nothing to do with religion. It is all about physiology, about Health and Well-being. Many people mistakenly believe that prayer and Meditation are associated with religious activities. Of course, they can be and sometimes are, however Meditation and Prayer are not the exclusive provinces of religion. Many people who have no religious affiliation are devoted to Meditation and prayer on a daily basis. There are several reputable scientific studies that provide solid information about the physical and psychological health benefits of Meditation and Prayer.

Benefits: Prayer purifies the heart and through Prayer, a believer attains spiritual devotion and moral elevation. Prayer not only gives a deep connection with God, but in prayer one establishes patience, humility, and sincerity. Prayer also provides a means of repentance and is a restrainer from shameful and unjust deeds. When you Meditate or pray, the activity of your brain moves from the right frontal cortex (where stress resides) to the calm left frontal cortex. Some mental benefits include greater creativity, decreased anxiety and depression, improved learning and memory, and increased happiness and emotional stability. Praying a few times a day engages the believer in constant remembrance of God and keeps him away from any unjust acts. It is through prayer that one can really find inner peace and fulfillment.

By praying we can find: a source of patience, courage, hope, confidence, inner peace, stability, equality, unity and an expression of the thankfulness of God.

Vedic Tradition of Prayer:

All the members of a family should meet once a day for family prayer. God's blessings come to the family that prays daily as a unit. By daily family prayer humility, good conduct, and love for God become apparent and mutual affection, goodwill and a cooperative spirit lead to family solidarity.

All the members of the family, regardless of size or age, should participate in prayer at a convenient time. Visitors and servants present should also be included. Everyone should assemble after washing their hands and face, then sit or stand in a convenient posture with the palms of the two hands clasped in a "Namaste" position. A lamp should then be lit and with quietness and peace of mind, the prayers should be said in a sincere and solemn manner. The prayer set out here are: Universal Prayer; Family Welfare Prayer; Meal time Prayer; Arti and Shanti Path Prayer; and Prayers for the improved health of any sick member of the family.

21

Chapter 4

Yoga Meditation: History and Origins

In the Yogic culture, Shiva is not known as a god, but as the Adi-Yogi (first Yogi) and the originator of Yoga or Meditation. Shiva was the one who first put this Bija into the human mind. According to Yogic lore, over 15,000 years ago, Shiva attained full enlightenment and abandoned himself to an intense and ecstatic dance upon the Himalayas. When his ecstasy allowed him some movement he would dance wildly. Other times when it passed beyond action, he would become utterly still.

Many saw he was experiencing something unknown previously and unfathomable which created interest and people gathered to see and know what he was doing. Shiva was oblivious to their presence and most soon left having grown weary of waiting for some explanation from him. During this time, he would either be in an intense dance, or absolute stillness. Finally, only seven men remained who's interest neither waned, or was lost. For these seven were insistent on learning and despite their pleas to Shiva, his disinterest remained constant. "Please, we want to know what you know," they cried in vain. His only reply was, "You fools. The way you are, you are not going to know in a million years. There is a tremendous amount of preparation needed for this. This is not entertainment."

The seven, still determined began to prepare. This preparation went on day after day, week after week, until finally on a full moon night after 84 years of Sadhana (Yogic practice) Shiva decided they were finally ready to receive instruction. After watching them closely, he waited for the next full moon to become a Guru (teacher). From this moment on he became the Adi-Guru (first teacher) and this day is known as Guru Purnima (teacher -full moon). After years passed these seven became fully, enlightened beings known today as the Saptarishis (seven sages)

Shiva, the Adi-Yogi, brought this possibility that proposes a human being need not be contained in the defined limitations of our species. There is a way to be contained in our physicality, but not be owned by it. We can inhabit the body, but never become solely the body. Also, there is a way to use the mind in the highest possible way, but still never know the miseries contained there. Finally, whatever dimensions of existence you find yourself in now can be surpassed and another way to live can be found. According to Shiva, "You can evolve beyond your present limitations if you do the necessary work upon yourself." Herein lies the significance of the Adi-Yogi.

Chapter 5

Types of Yoga (associated with Rishikesh Meditations

Raja Yoga (also called Ashtanga Yoga)

"The science of Raja-Yoga, in the first place, proposes to give us such a means of observing the internal states. The instrument is the mind itself. The power of attention, when properly guided, and directed towards the internal world, will analyze the mind, and illumine facts for us. The powers of the mind are like rays of light dissipated; when they are concentrated, they illumine." Swami Vivekananda from, *Complete Book of Yoga*

Yoga Sutras or Patanjali Ashtanga Yoga

The Yoga Sutras of Patanjali succinctly outline the art and science of traditional Yoga Meditation for Self-Realization. Herein lies the process of systematically encountering, examining, and then transcending each of the various gross and subtle levels of false identity in the mind field until the jewel of the True Self comes shining through. Yoga means union and sutra means thread.

The goal of this rendition of the Yoga Sutras is to make the principles and practices more understandable and accessible. The descriptions attempt to focus on the practical suggestions of what to do to regulate the mind, so as to attain direct experience beyond the mind. In the Yoga Sutras, Patanjali prescribes adherence to eight limbs or steps (the sum of which constitute Ashtanga Yoga to quiet one's mine and achieve Kaivalya, or liberation. These Sutras form the theoretical and philosophical basis of Raja Yoga, and are considered to be the most organized and complete definition of this discipline.

Eight-fold path of self-realization by Maharishi Patanjali

Yamas (Social Discipline): Yama means restraint or abstention and contains five moral practices. The are:
- o   **Ahimsa – (non-violence)**
- o   **Satya – (truthfulness)**
- o   **Asteya – (non-stealing)**
- o   **Brahmacharya – (celibacy)**
- o   **Aparigraha – (non-acquisitiveness)**
- •   **Niyamas (Individual Discipline):** Rules of conduct towards oneself consist of certain disciplines which are both physical and mental and are five in number:
  - o   **Shaucha – (cleanliness)**
  - o   **Santosha – (contentment)**

- ○ **Tapas** – (austerity)
- ○ **Svadhyaya** – (self-study)
- ○ **Ishvara Pranidhana** – (surrender to God)

Asana (Postures): Asana means holding the body in a particular posture to bring stability to the body and mind. The practice of Asana brings purity in the tubular channels, firmness and vitality to the body and mind. Patanjali has stated that any posture which is steady and comfortable is termed as Asana (Sthir Sukham Asanam).

Pranayama (Breath Control): The literal meaning of Pranayama is Breath Control. The aim of practicing Pranayama is to stimulate, regulate, and harmonize vital energy of the body. Just as a bath is required for purfying the body, so also is Pranayama for purifying the mind. Patanjali prescribes observation of breathing processes as a practice of Pranayama.

Pratyahara (Discipline of the Senses): The extroversion of the sense organs due to their craving after worldly objects has to be restrained and directed inwards towards the source of all existence. This process of drawing the sense inwards is Pratyahara, or putting the senses under restraint.

Dharana (Concentration): Dharana means focusing the pure mind on one's personal deity or on the individual self. The practice of Dharana helps the mind to concentrate on a particular object.

Dhyana (Meditation): When one sustains and maintains the focus of attention through Dharana unbound by time and space, it then becomes Shyana. Deep concentration destroys the Rajas and Tamas Gunas of mind and develops the Satvika Gunas (qualities).

Samadhi (Self-Realization): The eighth and final stage of Yoga is Samadhi. At this stage, one's identity becomes both externally and internally immersed in Meditation. The Meditator, the Act of Meditation, and the object Meditated upon all shed their individual characteristics and merge with one single vision of the entire Cosmos. Supreme happiness free from pleasure, pain and misery are experienced. Samadhi is the climax of Dhyana.

(See Diagram in the Pictorial Guide Section page 89)

Structure of the Yoga-sutra

First Chapter: Samadhi Pada – There are 51 Sutras in this chapter explaining about enlightenment

Second Chapter: Sadhana Pada – There are 55 Sutras in this section containing instructions about practice

Third Chapter: Vibhuti Pada – There are 56 Sutras about supra-normal powers (Siddhis) acquired by this practice

Fourth Chapter: Kaivalyapada (Liberation) This section of 34 Sutras describes the process of liberation and the reality of the transcendental ego.

See a detailed breakdown which includes English/Sanskrit definitions in the Pictorial Guide page 91

Hatha Yoga:

In Yoga, life and consciousness are known as Prakriti and Purusha. In Tantra they are called Shakti and Shiva. In Hatha Yoga they are called Ida and Pingala. In Taoism they are known as Yin and Yang. In Physics, these are called matter and energy. Names and perceptions vary with different philosophies. The concept of Hatha Yoga is to bring about a harmony between these two opposite polarities known as Ida and Pingala.

On the physical level this is defined as achieving the balance between sympathetic and parasympathetic nervous systems through the practice of various Asanas (postures) and Pranayama (Breath control) techniques. On a subtler level, the emphasis is on stimulation of the two Pranic pathways of the Ida and Pingala Nadis which run from the base of the spine (Muladhara Chakra) to the space between the eyebrows (Ajna Chakra). When the energies of the breath are balanced between Ida and Pingala, they merge, then enter the passageway at the base of the spine and rise as Kundalini. This action penetrates and awakens the Chakras while raising the Yogi to a higher state of consciousness.

Hatha Yoga is one of the ancient and significant Yogic techniques practiced by a large number of Yogis around the world. It is a preparatory process of Meditation and provides a path to attain a higher state of consciousness. Hatha is a combination of two Bija (seed) mantras Ha and Tha where Ha represents Prana, or the vital force, and Tha concerns the mind, or mental energy. Therefore, Hatha Yoga is the union of Pranic energy and mental actions . When these two are joined, awakening of the higher consciousness becomes known. The concept of Hatha Yoga is to bring about a harmony between Prakriti (nature) and Purusha (the self).

Hatha Yoga is also known as the Science of Purification. The body needs to be cleansed from different impurities. Removing these impurities allows the Nadis to function, energy blocks are released, and energy moves live wave frequencies through the channel to the brain. Therefore, Hatha Yoga is considered to be the preliminary practice of Raja Yoga, Kriya Yoga, and Kundalini awakening.

According to Swami Svatmaram, the main parts of Hatha Yoga are:
o   Asana

- ○ Shatkarma and Kumbhaka (Pranayama)
- ○ Bandhas and Mudra
- ○ Nad-anusandhana (Samadhi)
- ○

- **Sushumna-Ida-Pingla**

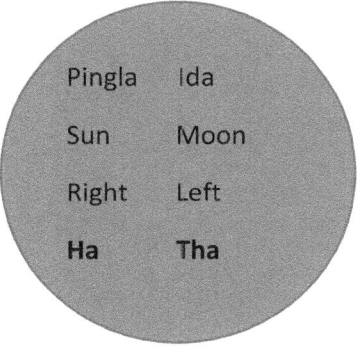

Pingla | Ida

Sun | Moon

Right | Left

Ha | **Tha**

Jnana Yoga:

Jnana in Sanskrit means knowledge and as used in the Bhagavad Gita is considered the path of Yoga dealing with the mind. Jnana Yogis consider wisdom and intellect as important and their aim is to unify the two to surpass limitations. This Yoga may be seen as practical in the fields of Philosophy and Metaphysics through both theory and practice. Jnana Yoga could be considered a quest for the Self by direct inquiry into who we are.

It is however, a mistake to think that the source could be found with the intellect alone. For purposes of self-discovery, Jnana Yoga probes the nature of the question, "Who am I." ((Ko Ham) Through persistent probing and fixing our attention on the source of our being, we regain our real Self. We remember who we are.

The inquiry, as the result of practicing Jnana Yoga leads us towards a clear awareness by removing our attention from that which we are not. Along with Bhakti Yoga (Devotion) Jnana Yoga is listed among the best approaches for becoming aware of the eternal Self (God). Shree Vasishtha and Shree Shankara are classical authorities on Jnana Yoga.

According to Swami Vivekananda from the *Complete Book of Yoga*, he says, "According to Advaita philosophy, there is only one thing real in the universe, which it calls Brahman; everything else is unreal, manifested and manufactured out of Brahman by the power of Maya. To reach back to that Brahman is our goal. We are, each one of us, that Brahman, that Reality, plus this Maya. If we can get rid of this Maya, or ignorance, then we become what we really are. According to this philosophy, each man consists of three parts – the body, the internal organ or the mind, and behind that, what is called the Atman, the Self. The body is the external coating and the mind is the internal coating of the Atman who is the real perceiver, the real enjoyer, the being in the body who is working the body by means of the internal organ or the mind."

Bhakti Yoga:

Bhakti Yoga is an intense devotion towards God. It is Prema of Prabhu, Sraddha and Visvas are the incipient stages of devotion which develop in Bhakti. Later, faith is the most important issue in the path of devotion. The qualifications for the attainment of Bhakti are a pure loving heart, faith, innocence, simplicity, truthfulness, Vairagya (detachment) and Brahmacharya (celibacy)

"Bhakti, says Narada in his explanation of the Bhakti-aphorisms, 'is intense love to God.' When a man gets it, he loves all, hates none; he becomes satisfied for ever." Swami Vivekananda from *Complete Book of Yoga*

Bhakti can be acquired and cultivated by constant Satsanga (associate with true people) devotees and repetition of his name: Sri Ram, Sita Ram, Hari Om, etc. Also by constant remembrance of the Lord through prayer, study of religious books; Ramayana, Hari Kirtan, service of Bhaktas which can infuse Bhakti in the heart. The following are all obstacles in the way of Bhakti Yoga: lust, anger, greed, pride, jealousy, hatred, egoism, desire for power, name and fame, and hypocrisy.

Japa Yoga

Japa is the repetition of any Mantra, or Name of the Lord. In this Kallyuga (period of strife/contention) Japa is an easy method for God-realization. Tukaram, Dhruva, Valmiki, Ramakrishna Paramahamsa, Narsi Mehta, Gauranga, Ramdas, Mira all had attained salvation by uttering the name of God which is a means for you to do also.

Mantras Deities:

- o   Om Ganesh Sharnam Sharnam Ganesha – Ganapati
- o   Om Namassivaya – Lord Siva
- o   Om Namo Narayanaya – Lord Narayana

- o   Sri Rama, Jaya Rama, Jaya Jaya Ram – Lord Rama
- o   Hare Rama Hara Rama, Rama Rama Hare Hare
- o   Hare Krishna Hara Krishna, Krishna Krishna Hare Hare – Mahamantra

Karma Yoga:

Karma means work or action. According to the Gita, any action is Karma. Charity, sacrifice, Tapas (ascetic practice) are all Karmas. In a philosophical sense, the following are all Karmas: breathing, seeing, hearing, tasting, feeling, smelling, walking, talking, etc. Thinking is the real Karma. Raga-Dvesha (attraction & repulsion) constitutes the real Karma. Half-hearted service is no service at all. Give your whole heart, mind, and soul when you serve. This is very important when you practice Karma Yoga.

"Karma in its effect on character is the most tremendous power that man has to deal with. Man is, as it were, a centre, and is attracting all the powers of the universe towards himself, and in this centre is fusing them all and again sending them off in a big current. Such a centre is the real man, the almighty, the omniscient, and he draws the whole universe towards him. Good and bad, misery and happiness, all are running towards him and clinging round him; and out of them he fashions the mighty stream of tendency called character and throws it outwards. As he has the power of drawing in anything, so has he the power of throwing it out." Swami Vivekananda from the *Complete Book of Yoga*

Life is very precious, therefore live in the spirit of the Gita's teaching and work without expectation of fruits and egoism. Think of yourself as Nimitta in the hands of Lord Narayana. If you work with this mental attitude you will become a Karma Yogi soon. Work never degrades a person and unselfish work is Puja (reverence/adoration) of Narayana. Work can be seen as worship and all works are sacred. There is no menial work from the highest view point; the place of the absolute; from the view point of Karma Yoga. If you work disinterestedly without any agency, then surrender the works and fruits as Ishvararpana (dedication/consecration to God) all Karmas are transformed into Yogic Kryas. Walking, eating sleeping, answering the calls of nature, speaking, etc. become offering unto the Lord. Every bit of work is Yoga for the practitioner. This is the central point for Nishkamya Karma Yoga. Every act can be spiritualized when the motive becomes pure, so serve everyone with intense love without any idea of agency without any expectation of frits or reward. Work is Meditation.

Chapter 6

Obstacles to Meditation

Pancha-Klesha: 5 Afflictions

The Yoga Sutras of Maharishi Patanjali describe five maladies that afflict every material being known as:
o   Avidya (Ignorance)
o   Asmita (Egoism)
o   Raga (Cravings)
o   Dvesha (Aversions)
o   Abhinivesha (Clinging to life)

> The lack of awareness of Reality, the sense of egoism or "I-am-ness," attractions and repulsions towards objects (of the senses) and a strong desire for life are the great afflictions or causes of all miseries in life.

These Pancha-Kleshas are the motivating factors that drive humans to act to produce and perpetuate Karma. The Pancha-Kleshas are also considered to be the five roots of problems of human existence.

Avidya (Ignorance) is said to be the Mother Klesha from which all the others spring forth, and rightly so. The base from which all obstructions to positive growth arises is lack of knowledge. Why? If one is possessed of true knowledge (Sat), then one understands the unity in everything.

The Oneness of the Self and the Universe does not suffer from the afflictions of *Asmita (Ego).* The erroneous belief of an individual who is separate and self-originating arises out of ignorance.

From this faulty foundation of belief, one constructs an entirely illusionary world in which one sees themselves as separate from their surroundings, thereby developing a dualistic relationship with the world around them. This belief *creates*

31

Raga (craving) to make things from without part of their within. *Dvesha (aversion)* occurs to things from without which is not desired from within.

With this worldly view, one lacks the fundamental awareness of their true nature which is a basic awareness necessary for the evolution of the consciousness. Instead, in this ignorance, one becomes further and further bound to a material existence which is exemplified in an inability to separate oneself from from their physical existence. This in turn creates *Abhinivesha (desire to cling desperately to this life).*

These five inborn psychological dispositions (Pancha Klesha) are rooted in Chitta (the subconscious mind). Only through Pratiprasava (complete eradication of the subconscious) can the Pancha Klesha be dissolved.

For further information on the additional connections between KOSHA, KLESHA, TATTVA, TANMATRA, SENSES, ORGANS, AND PRANA SEE: THE WONDERS OF 5 IN THE PICTORIAL GUIDE ON PAGE 90

Pancha-Kosha – Five Material Sheaths

A Kosha (sheath) is a covering of the Self according to Vedanta philosophy. There are five Pancha Koshas, and they are often seen as much like the layers of an onion. They envelop the soul like concentric rings with each more subtle than the succeeding one. Each succeeding Kosha affects or controls the activity of the preceding Kosha. They are the following:

Anna-Maya Kosha – The first is known as the food sheath which is the gross, physical body. Here are found the five organs of perception (Ears, skin, eyes, tongue, nose) and the five organs of action. The Anna-Maya Kosha is called the food sheath because food or anna enabled it to come into being and is maintained by food, ultimately ending up as food or the constituents of food.

Prana-Maya Kosha – The vital air sheath. There are five vital airs that correspond to the five physiological function of the mind and body. They are called the five Pranas. Together they constitute the vital air sheath and are shown below:

Prana – moves down from the base of the throat to the navel and energizes all the Vayus (winds) which move from the navel to the throat.

Udana – moves primarily from throat up to the head

Apana – moves from the navel down to the floor of the pelvis

Samana – moves from the periphery of the body into the core

Vyana – moves from the core out to the periphery

These five Pranas are sharp and clear in a person's youth, then with age they begin to lose their strength and vitality. This is why sight, hearing, etc. begin to fade with time and also the faculties of excretion, digestion and circulation become weak in old age. Our capacity to absorb and accept new thoughts and ideas is also reduced as we age.

Mano-Maya Kosha – This Kosha is known as the mind sheath and is comprised of: passions, emotions, thoughts, and impulses. It is filled with likes, as well as dislikes. The Mano-Maya Kosha controls the vital air and food sheaths. For example, when the mind is disturbed the Pranas (physiological functions) and the physical body are affected.

Vigyana-Maya Kosha – Is known as the Intellect sheath which thinks, reflects, reasons, discriminates, and judges. This Kosha analyses and distinguishes between pairs of opposites and controls the previous three sheaths.

Ananda-Maya Kosha – Is referred to as the Bliss sheath which consists of only mental impressions or tendencies in seed form call Vasanas. When you enter a deep and dreamless sleep all of your mental agitations cease, and undisturbed peace and bliss is experienced.

For further information on the additional connections between KOSHA, KLESHA, TATTVA, TANMATRA, SENSES, ORGANS, AND PRANA THE WONDERS OF 5 IN THE PICTORIAL GUIDE ON PAGE 90

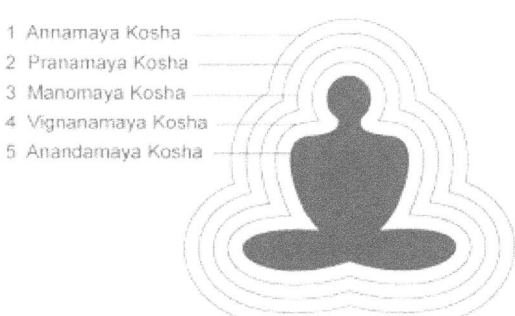

1 Annamaya Kosha
2 Pranamaya Kosha
3 Manomaya Kosha
4 Vignanamaya Kosha
5 Anandamaya Kosha

Tri-Gunas – Three Qualities of Maya

Every material living being is constantly undergoing the constant fluctuations of the three Gunas (attributes of nature) of Maya:

- o   Sattva – Darkness, Destruction, Death
- o   Rajas – Energy, Passion, Birth
- o   Tamas – Goodness, Purity, Light

We experience these as part of our Prarabdha Karma (past actions affecting the current life) in the form of Sanskaras (mental fluctuations) that affect our mood, understanding, behavior and desires in the form of environmental changes in the world around us.

Conclusion: The science of unhappiness gives us the tools to understand the kinds and types of Maya mentioned above that affect us all. Fortunately, the scriptures of Hinduism, the teachings of Saints and Bhakti philosophy tell us it's possible to eliminate the influence of all of these forever, and attain our ultimate aim of perfect divine bliss.

Chapter 7

Energy Centers

Chakras

Chakras, meaning Wheel, are psychic centers that lie along the axis of the spine as consciousness potentials. The are usually represented as a Lotus. The Chakras are not materially real and are to be understood as situated not in the gross body, but in the subtle, or theric body. They are repositories of psychic energies which govern the whole condition of being. What is most commonly known is a more recent system dating to around the Eight century C.E. with the main Seven Chakras. But the ancient spiritual Indian texts refer to various other systems with variation in the number of Chakras and their location.

When Kundalini is struck she awakens, uncoils, and begins to rise upwards like a fiery serpent that breaks upon each Chakra as she ascends until the Shakti merges with Shiva in the Sahasrara Chakra.

As Kundalini reaches each Chakra, tha particular Lotus opens and lifts its flower. As soon as she leaves for a higher Chakra, the Lotus closes its petals and hangs down symbolizing the activation of the energies of the Chakra and their assimilation to Kundalini. The dynamization of Kundalini when it passes from one Chakra to another is an unlding of spiritual consciousness stage by stage, and is said to enable the acquiring of Yogic powers called Siddhis.

The increasing number of Lotus petal in ascending order, may be taken to indicate the rising energy or vibration frequencies of the respective Chakras where each functions as a transformer of energies from one potency to another. Each of the 50 petals of the first Six Chakras are associated with one of the letters of the Sanskrit alphabet.

Each of the Chakras according to the Tantras corresponds to one of the elements of which the known world is compounded. Muladhara represents solidity; Svadhisthana is liquidity; Manipura is the gaseous; Anahata is the aerial; Vishuddha is the etheric or space. One can see the whole process as a progressive transformation of the elements with an increaded volatility. Each of the elements of the first five Chakras are associated with a sound, while the last two are the universal OM:
o   Lam - Muldhara
o   Vam - Svadhisthana
o   Ram - Manipura
o   Yam - Anahata
o   Ham.- Vishuddha
o   Om – Ajna

o   Om - Sahasrara

This ascent through the Chakras can be viewed as an upward journey through the self which refines and subtilizes the energy that is the Kundalini until at the Sic Chakra, the Ajna, or center of command where a qualitiative change has taken place. The Chakras are centers of transormation of psychic or mental energy into spiritual energy.

Note: See the Illustration in the Pictorial Guide on page 131 for a more detailed breakdown of each of the Seven Chakras.

Kundalini

According to the philosophy of Tantra, the entire universe is a manifestation of pure consciousness. In manifesting the universe, this pure consciousness seems to become divided into two poles or aspects neither of which can exist without the other. Each requires the other in order to manifest its total nature. One aspect,

Shiva is masculine and retains a static quality and remains identified with unmanifested consciousness. Shiva has the power to be but not the power to become or change.

The other aspect, Shakti, is feminine, dynamic, energetic, and creative. Shakti is the Great Mother of the universe for it is from her that all form is born.

According to Tantra, human beings are a miniature universe and all that is found in the cosmos can be found within each individual. The same principles that apply to the universe apply in the case of the individual being.

In human beings, Shakti the feminine aspect is called Kundalini. This potential energy is said to rest at the base of the spinal cord. The object of the Tantric practice of Kundalini Yoga is to awaken this cosmic energy and make it ascend through the psychic centers known as the Chakras which lie along the axis of the spine as consciousness potentials. She will then unite above the crown of the head with Shiva, the pure consciousness. This union is the aim of Kundalini Yoga to create a resolution of duality into unity again; a fusion with the Absolute. By this union the adept attains liberation while living which is considered in the Indian life to be the highest experience. A union of the individual with the universe. Once Kundalini Shakti has ascended to above the crown of the head and merged with Shiva it is made to reverse its course and return to rest at the base of the spine.

In Tantrism, the state of ultimate bliss is a transcendence of dualities male-female, energy-consciousness, and Shiva-Shakti

See the Illustration of Kundalini Energy in the Pictorial Guide on page 134

Section II: Practical Applications

Chapter 8

Shatkarmas (Purification Techniques)

Shatkarmas, or Purification techniques are one of the Kriyas (practices) from the Hatha Yoga Pradipika help the Yoga practitioner by cleansing the body of impurities and toxic substances which then improves the Pranic flow of energy. There are six in all, but only the simple ones can be practiced by the student without the proper tutoring of a Guru. Those more complex can be learned under the careful guidance of an experienced teacher such as Dhauti,(alimentary canal), Nauli (abdomen), and Basti (large intestine). Included in this text are Ushapan, Sneezing, Jala Neti, Amla eyewash, and Trataka (more information can be found on Trataka in the Meditation's section.

Ushapan:

Ushapan basically refers to drinking water when you get up. In the word Ushapan, Usha (means Dawn) and Pan (means to drink). The first thing a normal person would do after waking from sleep is to brush the teeth, or answer nature's call, but to optimize the saliva one should drink 1-2 glasses of water upon rising. This would be for those who would be at work within 1-2 hours after waking, however for those whose employment does not call for them to leave for several (3-4) hours, then 3-4 glasses would be optimal. It is normally recommended that elders and children should take about two glasses and the middle aged should consume 3-4 glasses of water prior to brushing the teeth.. The reasoning for this practice is when we sleep our stomach acidifies a little due to enzymes and the saliva has these present after a long sleep period. This precious commodity assists in digestion and can aid the user. The recommended procedure is to drink the water in sips, being sure to swirl the water around the inside of the mouth, instead of in one gulp to be sure as much as possible is absorbed. The recommended procedures are:

Heat the water to a lukewarm temperature
Store the water overnight in a copper vessel and consume daily

Benefits of Ushapan:

Helps in combating many diseases, and the most probable is how it leads to proper discharge of waste from the body. The daily use of Ushapan may assist with the following:

Headaches
Problems with blood pressure

Hyperacidity
Rheumatism
Obesity
Constipation
Diabetes
Eye diseases
Coughs
Kidney stones
Improved health

Sneezing:

Sneezing is a sudden, forceful, uncontrolled burst of air through the nose and mouth. It is one of our protective reflexes and occurs when something irritates the inside of our nose. Tiny nerve ending in the nostrils send a message to our brain, which in turn sends signals to numerous parts of the body to facilitate this reaction. During the act of sneezing, the chest muscles compress the lungs which send a burst of air upwards constricting the throat, forcing air to exit through the mouth and nostrils. The nose acts as a filter to eliminate germs, bacteria, and other foreign substances during the sneezing process. Afterwards, the nostrils are cleansed allowing a free flow of air aiding the breathing process.

A common paper napkin can be used for this technique according to the following steps.
 Unfold the napkin until all four sections are displayed. Cut/Tear into individual sections Begin at one corner and begin to fold the section until the opposite end is reached. This should appear as a tight, flat length of paper.

Beginning at the middle point of the tube, begin to tightly wind the tube in one direction. There should be a long, thin, wiry point appearing at the end when you are done. Then turn the tube and do the same to the other side.

Tear this tube into equal halves. Find a comfortable place and take a standing position. Lean slightly forward and using the first of these sneezing aids, carefully insert the sharp end into the nostril until a tickling sensation is noticed. This may require some practice until your sneezing spot is located. Use a gentle probing motion, but to not twirl the end inside the nostril.

With practice you should be able to sneeze several times. If you have difficulty in making yourself sneeze, then keep trying until the proper spot is located within the nasal cavity.

Sneezing should be done on a daily basis as part of the Purification process.

JALA NETI: Nasal Cleansing with Saline Water

Jala Neti is a Yogic technique to clean your sinuses. Neti is one of the six Shatkarmas (purification methods) in Hatha Yoga. The sinus cavities can get clogged with impurities which may then cause infections, inflammations, and headaches. The Yogic text: Hatha Yoga Pradeepika gives a simple method to keep your sinuses clean. Also, there are six practices for cleansing the body, thereby preparing it and the mind for higher practices of Yoga within the pages of this text.

One of these practices is called Neti and deals with nasal hygiene and can be linked to many conditions such as:
Sinusitis
Migraines
Headaches
Allergies
Asthma

Neti is a very simple practice which can be done along with your daily routine after brushing the teeth after wakening. This practice takes only a few minutes and helps to relieve many of the health issues related to the nasal and sinus cavities.

To do Jala Neti begin with lukewarm saline water, a Neti Pot, and plain table salt. A Neti Pot is a small pot with a long spout on the side which is inserted into one of the nostrils during the practice. This pot can be made of copper, steel, ceramic, or plastic and can be found in most health, drug, or natural food stores. Water is the most common liquid used and is referred to as Jala Neti, however milk can also be used and would be called Dugdha Neti.

In order to complete Jala Neti the following is a step by step procedure:
Have two liter sized containers, a level tablespoon of salt, and hot distilled water. Pour the hot water into the container, but do not add the salt. Next, pour additional cold distilled water into the container a little at a time until the water has reached a lukewarm stage in temperature. You can test the water by pouring a little over your fingers until it reaches the desired temperature. (Water must not be too hot, or too cold, or irritation of the sinuses can occur) Once you have this to your satisfaction it is time to add the salt.

A tablespoon of salt is enough for approximately 8 people. If this is being done for a single person, then reduce the amount by 1/8th teaspoon per person using a reduced amount of water. Too much salt in the mixture can cause severe irritation of the nasal passages.

Steps for the Jala Neti practice:before beginning it is important to be aware of your Ha and Tha breath. This is done by testing your exhalation from each nostril. First using the index finger of either hand, press and close one of the nostrils and exhale through the opposite nostril. Do this for both nostrils and see if one is clearer than the other when exhaling. Begin with the nostril where breath is exhaled easier. Be sure to have napkins, tissue, or a cloth to help in blowing the nose after the procedure is completed.

Pour the saline water into the Neti Pot and place the spout into the selected nostril firmly to avoid leakage.
Be sure to be slightly bent over, tilt the head to the opposite side to create a direct line for water to flow down to the opposing nostril. Be sure to allow the water to flow to a place on the ground.

The mouth should be slightly open, and breathing should be done by the mouth since the nose is engaged in cleansing.

Do this procedure for both nostrils as many times as you feel necessary to insure a proper cleansing practice.

There may some effects such as sneezing, irritations, coughing, etc. in the beginning of this practice, but they will disappear after a few sessions.

Benefits of Jala Neti:

Helps to maintain the nasal hygiene by removing the dirt and bacteria trapped along with the mucus in the nostrils.

De-sensitizes the tissues inside the nose, which can help to alleviate rhinitis, allergies, and some asthmas.

Health problems like sinusitis, migraine, headaches, ear problems like Tinitis, and middle ear infections can be reduced.

Alleviate upper respiratory complaints, sore throats, tonsillitis, and dry coughs

Help to clear the eye ducts and improve vision

Aids the mind by removing tension, depression, and provide mental clarity

Associated practices of Neti

Neti or Nasal cleaning can also be done with milk and is called Dhugdha Neti. There is another practice called Sutra Neti where a waxed cotton string is inserted into the nose and pulled out from the mouth. Cleaning is done by a back and forth motion of the string. Instead of using cotton thread, a rubber catheter may also be used which can be readily found in drug stores. The benefits of Sutra Neti are similar to that of Jala Neti.

Amla Eye Wash

Stir the Amla powder in distilled water in a small glass container using a level teaspoon, mix well, then cover and let sit overnight for use the next morning. (Note: if not used within the 24 hour period create a new batch) Prior to use, be sure to stir the mixture again, use a strainer to remove any sediment and dilute by adding an additional 50% of distilled water.

Fill eye cups to three-quarters level and place these to the eyes (which are closed) in a slightly bent over position with the eye cups snug against the eye sockets

Blink the eyes rapidly for just a moment, then move the eyes in a circular motion to expose the eyes completely. open the eyes to half position. Finally, open the eyes completely saturating them completely. Blot gently with tissue to dry.

Trataka (Focused Gazing)

Focused gazing is covered in more detail in the Practical section under Meditations. The benefits of focused gazing are increasing strength in the eye muscles, improved focus, and increased circulation to the eyes. Please see page 78 for steps in practicing Trataka using a candle for the object of intentional gazing. However, Trataka can be performed by looking at one's reflection in the mirror, being outside in nature with rivers, mountains, or other objects

Yantra (Focused Gazing on a Geometrical Design)

Yantra, much like Trataka uses geometric designs and an unblinking gaze to increase the ability to focus attention and to create a sense of deep silence and rest. By practicing Yantra, practitioners can develop the Ajna (Third Eye) where the psychic powers reside. . Yantra Meditation is discussed more in depth in the practical section on Meditations..

Chapter 9

Pranayama

Introduction to Breathing and Life Force

The Sanskrit term Pranayama comprises two components known as Prana (life force) and Ayama (extension). Therefore, the word Pranayama literally translates as the extension of the life force. The inhalation and exhalation of breath purifies and cleanses an individual and can calm the agitated mind or energize the overexerted body.

Breathing is a bridge between the body and mind. A common occurrence when meditating is to have tension in the muscles and a mind filled with chatter. The nervous system may be seen as that which sits in judgement between these two essential parts of the human body. One of the best ways to regulate the nervous system, and consequently the body and mind, is through control of the breath. For thousands of years, Yogis have known this to be true. In today's society, there is acceptance of this by professionals from both the medical and psychological community.

Four Parts of Breath:
Inhalation ———►   Hold ————► Exhalation ————►
(A.K)   (B.K)

There are different qualities of breathing which may be seen as general and personal as they apply to the individual. Two are very obvious: Puraka (inhalation) and Rechaka (exhalation). However, there are two others, and these are known as Kumbhaka, which would be the hold, or stops after breathing. The hold after Puraka (the inhalation) is called Antah Kumbhaka (A.K), and the hold after Rechaka (exhalation) is called Bahya Kumbhaka (B.K.)

Witnessing Natural Breath

First, begin a conscious analysis of your breathing right now. Close the eyes and a take a moment to observe your breath as you mentally answer the following:
- o   Are you inhaling through your nose, or the mouth?
- o   Does your chest and stomach expand, or contract when breathing?
- o   Is the inhalation traveling deeply into the abdomen, or end in the chest?
- o   What feelings are present as oxygen enters and exits the body?

Three Keys to Starting a Pranayama Practice:

Before beginning a Pranayama practice keep these three factors in mind:

- o   The length of your breath
- o   The breathing ratio
- o   A suitable breathing technique

A core teaching in Pranayama is that a practice should focus on lengthening Rechaka (exhalation) knowing that Puraka (inhalation) will follow with a rule of thumb being developing a breathing ratio where the exhalation should be equal to, or longer than the inhalation.

When beginning the practice of Pranayama, remember that enhancing the overall energy of the body does not only occur when feeling invigorated. At times, calming down is the best way to focus and regenerate your energy. Performing various Pranayama exercises described later in this text will all you to become more insightful and provide a rejuvenation of energy.

Special Breathing Practices:
Diaphragmatic Breathing:

Diaphragmatic breathing is one of the most important foundation practices for Meditation. When the diaphragm is used for breathing, there is motion in the lower abdomen as it rises, while the chest remains still. Too often in today's stress filled lives, we develop poor habits when it comes to the natural occurrence of breathing which in turn create tension in the mind and body. It is important to develop good diaphragmatic breathing since without this practice, the progress in Meditation as a spiritual pursuit will be hindered.

Yogic Breathing (Complete Breath)

Though not performed in a vigorous way, the Complete Breath is extremely invigorating by involving the abdomen, diaphragm, and chest muscles. This is done by breathing sequentially in the following steps:

- o   First inhale completely at the abdomen.
- o   Second, continue to inhale by filling the mid-section where the diaphragm resides.
- o   Third, continue to inhale by filling the chest which allows the upper chest and shoulders to rise.
- o   Finally, systematically release and empty from the upper portion of the body, then move to the mid-section, and finally empty completely the abdomen. The Complete Breath is good to do whenever one is Meditating. The simple act of 3-5 breaths will have a useful and invigorating effect.

Spinal Breathing

There are a variety of practices with awareness moving up and down the spine with breathing. One may do this practice between particular Chakras (energy centers), or form different shapes of the visualized flow. The most straight forward, complete method is to:

o   Imagine the breath flowing from the top of the head in a downward motion to the base of the spine on exhalation.
o   Then, imagine the flow coming from the base of the spine to the top of the head on inhalation.
o   Spinal Breathing can be done in an easy seated position, or in Shavasana (lying down)
o   As this process is in progress, one may simply experience the breath, or visualize a thin, milky white stream of energy flowing in a straight line, either in an upwards, or downwards motion. The practice is very subtle when experienced at its depth and can turn into a profoundly deep part of the Meditation practice.

Breath Awareness:

The entire science of breath begins with awareness of what the breath is doing. To do this means having an attitude of an explorer, or possibly an interior researcher. Doing so means cultivating an attitude of curiosity allowing the explorer to wander inside of themselves with an awareness of how the breath operates.

Awareness of the feel of the breath at the bridge of the nostrils is a very simple, straight forward and highly effective Meditation practice. This can be seen as a cognitive sense of touch, or of the air which is literally felt coming and going. Allowing the breath to slow on exhalation is a further refinement where exhalation is twice as much in duration as inhalation. For an enhanced experience, allow there to be no pause between the breaths as exhalation gently flows into inhalation, then inhalation gently flows into exhalation. This particular practice is excellent preparation for the subtler, ore advanced practices.

Chapter 10

Pranayama: Techniques

Kapalbhati Pranayama (Skull Shining Breathing Exercise):

Kapalbhati (or Kapalabhati) is one of the six Shatkarmas (methods of purification in Hatha Yoga). In Sanskrit "Kapal" means the skull and "Bhati" means to shine or illuminate. Kapalbhati cleans the cranial sinuses and hence the name. Some include Kapalbhati as of of the Pranayama, but in the classic Yogic texts, *Hatha Yoga Pradeepika* and *Gheranda Samhita*, it is classified in the Shatkarmas.

Kapalbhati is a breathing technique where the exhalation (Rechaka) is forceful and rapid, while the inhalation (Puraka) is normal. Exhalation is the main part of this practice. The foreceful exhalation throws out the stale air from the lungs and the deep inhalation increases the oxygen content in the bloodstream with the resultant effect of purifying the nerves and the pranic nadis. Kapalbhati also removes the excess of Kapha (one of the three Doshas in Ayurveda) from the body.

Kapalbhati has to be practiced in a very steady posture such as Padmasana (Lotus pose),Siddhasana (Accomplished pose), and Vajrasana (Thunderbolt pose) with hands resting on the knees.

In normal breathing, inhalation is the active process while exhalation is passive. In Kapalbhati this is reversed. The abdominal muscles and the diaphragm are used to forecefully exhale the air. The abdominal muscles forcefully move inwards towards the diaphragm thereby throwing the air out. The inhalation is done in a passive relaxed way to fill the lungs with fresh air. This is practiced without any gap between the two respirations.

All Pranayama practices should be learned under the guidance of a qualified Yoga Meditation instructor.

Also, if you have any medical condition please consult your attending physician before taking up the practice. Kapalbhati should not be practiced by those suffering from heart ailments, high blood pressure, stroke or epilepsy. Those with ulcers should do this Pranayama with caution. If you have and any recent surgery of the thorax and abdomen, avoid the practice entirely.

Steps for Practice:

Kapalbhati has to be practiced on an empty stomach. Early morning and evening are the best time for your practice, but ensure there has been a span of at least four (4) hours since the last meal.

To perform Kapalbhati, sit in a steady posture using those Asanas mentioned above. Next:

Place the hands on the knees and breathe normally.

Relax the entire body and ensure the back is straight, long neck, and chin parallel to the floor.

Breathe in and out rapidly with the exhalation being forceful. The inhalation should be passive and normal. During exhalation the belly goes inside towards the thorax, forcing out the air from the lungs. Inhalation is done with relaxation to fill the lungs again with fresh air.

Initially one can start with 60 rounds in one minute. Each inhalation and exhalation should take approximately second. Subsequently, with enough practice, increase the speed to 120 rounds per minute. Here, each inhalation and exhalation takes only half a second. Increasing the speed beyond this may not be useful as the breathing will become very shallow.

After the number of rounds, relax and breathe normally till the breathing rate comes back to normal. The relaxation period can be roughly between 30 seconds to one minute.

Repeat this process about 3 times in the initial stages. For example, if you are practicing at a rate of 60 rounds per minute, then you would have completed a total of 180 rounds (insure there is a rest between every 60 rounds). This completes one sitting, however you may have multiple Kapalbhati sessions: one in the morning and one in the evening.

Practice of Kapalbhati with the Three Bandhas:

Advanced practioners can practice Kapalbhati along with the three Bandhas (energy locks). The Bandhas will be covered later in the text in greater detail.

Ujjayi Pranayama (Psychic Breath)

Ujjayi Pranayama or the psychic breath soothes the mind and induces a meditative state. Ujjayi means to lift up. In Ujjay Pranayama, the chest is slightly lifted up as if the inhalation is done from the throat. Ujjayi involves a deep inhalation from both nostrils with a half-closed glottis which creates a faint, hissing, snoring sound during inhalation. Then, there is a retention of breath followed by exhalation. **Those suffering from heart ailments and blood pressure conditions should avoid Kumbhaka, or retention of breath.**

Steps for Practice:

Sit in a comfortable Meditative pose. (Padmasana, Siddhasana, Swastikasana, Sukhasana, Vajrasana) Ujjayi breathing may even be performed during light activities such as sitting and walking.

Contract the glottis so the passage of the throat is partially shut.

Roll the tongue up and let the lower side of the tongue touch the upper palate.

Breathe in slowly through the throat making a slight hissing, snoring sound. During inhalation the chest is slightly lifted up and the abdomen contracts slightly.

When the inhalation is complete, swallow the breath and perform Jalandhara Bandha (chin lock).

Retain the breath inside for as long as you are comfortable. In the initial stages, Kumbhaka (breath retention) can be avoided. Add this to the practice when you feel comfortable holding the breath.

Release the Jalandhara Bandha (Chin lock) and exhale through the Ida Nadi (left nostril), Block the right nostril with the right thumb during exhalation. Exhalation may also be done through both nostrils. This completes one round of Ujjayi Pranayama. Perform as many rounds as possible depending on your comfort level.

Bhastrika Pranayama (Bellows Breath)

Bhastrika Pranayama is one of the main forms of Pranayama. In Sanskrit, Bhastrika means Bellows and just as the Blacksmith blows his bellows to create hat and purify iron, Bhastrika is said to purify the mind and clear Pranic blocks. Bhastrika involves both rapid inhalation as well as exhalation, which helps to increase the circulation of blood in the entire body. During rapid and forced exhalation the chest is compressed thereby pushing the blood towards the head. During the inhalation, the reverse takes place. This process increases the blood flow to every part of the body increasing the vitality of all the organs and tissues. The long term practice of Bhastrika purifies the body and awakens the inherent higher powers plus increasing the oxygen content in the blood.

Those suffering from the following should avoid the practice of Bhastrika:
o   **Heart Disease**
o   **Acute Asthma**
o   **Fever**
o   **Recent surgeries**
•   **The practice of Bhastrika can be a little intense for some and should be learned under the guidance of a qualified Yoga Meditation Instructor. In case of any existing medical conditions, please consult with your attending physician before beginning the practice of Bhastrika.**

Steps to Practice:

Begin by sitting in a comfortable Asana (mentioned previously). Keep the body erect and close the mouth.

Inhale and exhale in rapid succession. During this process a hissing sound is produced. Begin by 10 inhalations and exhalations per round which can be increased over a period of time. Some practitioners reach the point where they begin to perspire.

Bhastrika can be performed with Kumbhaka (breath holding) at the end of the last exhalation. To do this take a deep breath after the last exhalation and hold the breath inside for as long as comfortable. Then, exhale and start breathing normally. This will constitute one round.

Perform three such rounds of Bhastrika Pranayama. Between rounds, rest for a short period until breathing returns to normal. If short of time, practice at least one round which is sufficient to maintain fitness.

Bhastrika can be done once in the morning and again in the evening (if the temperature is cool).

Anulom Vilom Pranayama (Alternate Nostril Breathing)

Anulom Vilom Pranayama, or alternate nostril breathing, is one of the main practices of Pranayama. In the practice of Pranayama, Puraka (inhalation) and Kumbhaka (retention) are used. Anulom Vilom Pranayama can be practiced with or without Kumbhaka. Beginners should begin the practice without Kumbhaka. The duration of inhalation and exhalation depends entirely on the capacity of the practitioner. However, one should begin at their own comfort level.

In Anulom Vilom Pranayama is done only through one nostril which is then alternated. During the practice the opposite nostril is closed using the fingers. The thumb is used to close the right nostril and the ring finger is used to close the left
nostril. The Anulom Vilom Mudra is shown in the Pictorial section of this text and is used for performing this Pranayama.

The purpose of Pranayama is to control the breathing mechanism which is an involuntary process. Breathing goes on even in our sleep as it is controlled by the central nervous system. With the regular practice of Pranayama, this process can be brought into our conscious control to some extent. In the Yoga text: Hatha Yoga Pradeepika, the breath is compared to a wild animal. Jus as elephants, lions, and tigers can be controlled with a steady and prolonged training period, the Yogi also brings the breath under his control with constant practice.

Anulom Vilom Pranayama should be done on an empty stomach preferably in the morning after evacuation. It can also be done in the evening with a gap of 4 hours after the last meal.

Steps to Practice:

Sit in a steady asana such as Padmasana, however Siddhasana and Vajrasana may also be used.

Close the right nostril with your thumb and draw in air from the left nostril. Do this as slowly as you can until the lungs are full.

Next, release the thumb and close the left nostril with your ring finger. Then breathe out slowly through the right nostril.

Now, take the air in from the right nostril and release it through the left nostril (be sure to close the right nostril with the thumb) This completes Round 1 of Anulom Vilom Pranayama.

Start with 5 rounds and increase them up to 20 rounds in one sitting. The duration of inhalation can begin at 2 seconds and go up to 20 seconds or longer.

One can have a sitting in the morning and another in the evening. For advanced practitioners, the Yogic texts recommend four sittings: Morning (once); Noon (once);evening (once); Midnight (once)

However, for all practical purposes only 2 sittings of Anulom Vilom are sufficient. After the practitioner has reached a level of proficiency, Kumbhaka can be added to the practice.

Bhramari Pranayama: Humming Bee Breath

Bhramari Pranayama, or the Humming Bee Breath produces a sound similar to the humming of a bee. Bhramari comes from the Sanskrit word Bramar which means a kind of black Indian bee. Bhramari Pranayama has a soothing effect on the brain and calms the mind. In Bhramari Pranayama, the humming sound is produced during slow exhalation. The eyes and ears are closed using the fingers during this process. This cuts off external sense inputs of sound and sight helping to internalize the consciousness. Practice of Bhramari Pranayama can be a prelude to Nada Yoga, or the science of Meditation on internal sounds.

Steps to Practice:

Sit in a comfortable Meditative pose keeping the spine erect. Do not practice in Sevasana (Corpse pose) lying down.

Breathe normally and relax the entire body.

Keep the mouth closed and the teeth slightly apart.

Begin with the eyes closed and then use the index fingers, or thumbs to plug the ears.

Take a slow, deep inhalation and fill the lungs completely.

Next, exhale slowly making a continuous humming sound from the throat. The sound you hear should reverberate in the head and should approximate the same tone as that of a bee humming.

Focus on the sound vibrations in your skull maintaining awareness of the continuous drone the sound produces. This completes one round.

Begin with 5 rounds and increase it as per your convenience.

Chapter 11

Bandhas (Energy Locks) Uplifting Energy

Uddiyana Bandha (Abdominal Lock)

Uddiyana Bandha, or the Abdominal Lock is one of the three main Bandhas (Locks) practiced by Yogis. Uddiyana Bandha is said to activate the Manipuraka Chakra and channels the Pranic energy upwards.

Uddiyana Bandha is practiced by pulling the abdomen inwards after exhalation and holding the breath outside (Bahya Kumbhaka). In this Bandha, the abdominal muscles press the organs in the abdomen against the wall behind the organ which is next to the spinal column.

Uddiyana Bandha is to be practiced after the practice of Asanas and Pranayamas, but before starting any Meditation practices. Gheranda Samhita calls Uddiyana Bandha the Lion that slays the Elephant of Death. Uddiyana Bandha may also be practiced along with Pranayama and Mudras.

Uddiyana Bandha should be practiced after Agnisara Kriya (Stomach Lift) which helps to loosen up the abdominal muscles before taking up the practice of Uddiyana Bandha. It should be done under the guidance of a teacher.

Those suffering from the following should not do Uddiyana Bandha:
o   **Blood pressure problems**
o   **Heart Diseases**
o   **Ulcers of the stomach and intestine**
o   **During pregnancy**

Uddiyana Bandha can also be practiced in Inverted Poses, but guidance and practice is suggested

Steps to Practice:

Sit in Padmasana or Siddhasana with the spine straight

Place the palms on the knees while breathing normally,and relax the whole body.

Inhale deeply and then exhale fully.

Hold the breath outside (Bahya Kumbhaka), then slightly bend the shoulders, and lean forward.

Perform Jalandhara Bandha (Chin Lock) and press down the knees with the palms.

55

Contract the abdominal muscles and pull them inside and upwards. Imagine as if there is a suction from a point just behind the sternum. This will enable the abdomen to go fully inside while pressing all the abdominal organs against the back wall of the spine.

Hold the lock with the breath outside for as long as you are comfortable. Once can start with a few seconds, then gradually increase it to a minute over a period of time. Experts can hold the breath outside for two minutes or more.

To release the lock, first release the abdominal muscles. Then bring the shoulders back to normal position, then finally release the chin lock and inhale.

Wait till your breathing process comes back to normal. This precess can be repeated as many times as you are comfortable.

Moola Bandha (Root Lock):

Moola Bandha/Mula Bandha, or the Root Lock is one of the three main Bandhas, or Yogic Locks practiced by Yogis. Moola in Sanskrit means Root and Bandha means lock. It is said to activate the Mooladhara Chakra which then stimulates the Kundalini Shakti at the base of the spine.

Moola Bandha is categorized as a Mudra or Yogic gesture in both the classical texts: Hatha Yoga Pradeepika and the Gheranda Samhita. As a Mudra it helps to channel Pranic energy in a certain way, but the terminology Bandha refers more to the energy lock that it creates.

Steps to Practice:

Stage 1:

Sit in Siddhasana, but women can use the Siddha Yoni Asana. In this Asana the left heel is pressed against the Perineum located close the anus and the right heel is placed on the genital organ.

Relax the whole body and breathe naturally while keeping the spine straight.

Gently contract the Perineal/Vaginal region and then release slowly. During contraction pull up the entire pelvic floor and then release. Do this slowly and rhythmically.

Repeat this as long as you are comfortable as you breathe normally during the practice.

Stage 2:

In Stage 1 the contraction involves the muscles of the Anal region, the perineum, and the urinary region. In Stage 2, the practitioner learns to separate out the Perineal muscles from the rest of the muscles in the pelvic region.
Try to contract just the Perineal/Vaginal muscles slowly. Hold this for a few seconds and then release them. Do this slowly and rhythmically. This is said to be the location of the Mooladhara Chakra.

Continue the practice till mastery is achieved before moving to Stage 3.

Stage 3:
In Stage 3 inhale deeply and hold the breath. Contract the Perineal/Vaginal muscles slowly and then hold tightly. This is the final stage of Moola Bandha.

Maintain the contraction for as long as you are comfortable. Remember you have your breath held inside (Antah Kumbhaka). Maintain the contraction only as long as you can hold the breath comfortably inside. Then release the breath along with the Perineal muscles.

Take a few breaths in between to relax. Repeat this process as many times as you are comfortable.

Stage 4:

Stage 4 should be practiced only by advanced seekers under guidance of a Yoga expert. In this stage the Perineal contraction is maintained for a prolonged period of time which can vary from a few minutes, to a few hours. During this process the breath is not held inside. Instead the practitioner can take slow and shallow breaths throughout the process while maintaining the contraction. During this process many hidden psychic patterns can be released and the practitioner should maintain a detached witness attitude.

General Knowledge:

Practice of Moola Bandha should be learned from a spiritual teacher. The practice can create an awakening of the lower psychic centers which can release a lot of sexual energy. The practitioner should have guidance from a competent spiritual Guru during this time to overcome the any obstacles encountered during the practice. The released energy should be effectively channeled to the higher psychic centers for spiritual growth, or else it may create mental problems for those practicing this Bandha.

During this practice many practitioners have difficulty correctly locating the Mooladhara Chakra. It is easy to find. For men, the muscles for contraction is between the Anus and the Testes. For women it is at the opening to the womb at a spot where the Uterus meets the vagina found behind the cervix. However, women should avoid practicing Moola Bandha during Menstruation periods.

During the initial stages, practitioners might find it difficult to separate out the Perineal muscles from the Anal and Genital muscles. This can be overcome by practicing Ashwini Mudra (Anal Contraction) and Vajroli Mudra (Genital Contraction) separately.

Chapter 12

Marma (Energy Points)

Throughout the body there are those energy points we are familiar with such as the Seven Chakras, however there are also 61 Marma Points of energy which can be used in Meditation. These can be compared to those found in Acupuncture/Acupressure which are normally stimulated using external devices such as needles, fingers, or others. These Marma points can be stimulated through the practice of intense concentration on each location in the body outlined in the body diagram **(shown in Pictorial Guide).** Point #1 is located at the forehead, circulating throughout the trunk, the arms and legs, and returning to the starting point at #1. During this Meditation, the intense focus on each point acts as a stimulus to activate energy much as an acupuncture needle does, or the external pressure applied.

Pratyahara (concentration) is developed by a sharp focus on each point, thereby stimulating the energy located there. Performing this 61-point focus on these energy points is a prelude to Yoga Nidra (Psychic Sleep) where the practitioner can enter the state beyond consciousness and unconsciousness. Stimulating Marma points also stimulates the Chakras and the various Doshas (Biological energies). Focusing your attention to the 61 points can improve your health, focus, and energy over time.

(See Pictorial Guide for detailed Marma Points Body Chart)

Steps to Practice:

To perform a 61 point Marma Meditation begin in Shavasana (Corps Pose) with arms at the sides and palms up.

Begin at point #1 located at the forehead by placing all of your focus on that point. Visualize a point of energy and hold your focus there.

Move down the body to the next point located at the neck which is a major transition point from the forehead to the trunk and arms. Points #2, 14, 26, and 60 are found here as well as the circuit is made from Head to Toe, and Toe to Head.

Continue down the right side at succeeding points until completed and then cross the trunk to the left side. Proceed until the left side is completed and a return has been made to point #61 (which is the same as #1)

At each point try to avoid distractions such as random thoughts, external noises, or any other which might lead you to lose focus. Do not be disappointed if this does not happen right away and will improve over time as you practice more frequently.

Chapter 13

Mudras (Seal, Gesture, Mark) For Meditation

Chin or Jnana Mudra (Gesture of Wisdom)

Chin/Jnana Mudra or Gyan Mudra is the most common Yogic Mudra used in Meditation. In Sanskrit, the word Jnana means knowledge or wisdom and Mudra means sign or gesture. It literally translates to the psychic gesture of knowledge or wisdom.

Benefits:

Chin/Jnana Mudra modifies the Pranic flow in the fingers. Usually the Prana flows out through the extremities (hands,feet, heat, etc.), however in Jnana Mudra some of the flow is redirected by joining the thumb and forefinger which has formed a circular loop. This sends mind energy inwards where it can be internalized, thereby calming the mind. Meditative Asanas make the body steady, while the Mudras add to the mental steadiness. Using this Mudra one can sit in Meditation for a long duration of time as it reduces mental distractions which arise. One can see the Jnana Mudra as a psychic-neural finger lock which helps to internalize the Prana.

Steps to Practice:

Chin/Jnana Mudra is used as a Meditative gesture done in any comfortable Meditation Asana (any mentioned previously). Please begin by:

Fold the index finger and let it touch the base of the thumb. The forefinger forms a circle, but the thumb points straight out.

Straighten the other three fingers gently.

Once this is done on both hands, place them on the knees with the palm facing upwards.

The three fingers should point forward and face up.

Adjust the position of the resting hands and relax the shoulders, spine straight, long neck, and chin parallel to the floor while practicing Meditation. Keep this position throughout the entire Meditation session you are practicing.

Variations of Jnana Mudra:

An equally common practice is to keep the tip of the forefinger touching the tip of the thumb causing them to form a complete circle.

Gyan Mudra is accomplished by facing the palm downwards.

Ashwini Mudra

Ashwini Mudra comes from the Sanskrit word Ashwa which means a horse and Mudra means gesture or sign. Ashwini Mudra should not be confused with Moola Bandha and Vajroli Mudra which also involves contraction of muscles below the abdominal region. Ashwini Mudra is very easy to perform and can be done during anytime of the day or night, and by any age group. This Mudra is performed by contracting the anal sphincter muscles in a rhythmic manner.

Steps to Practice:

The following steps should be done in order to perform the Ashwini Mudra:

Sit in a comfortable and Meditative pose as those mentioned previously. Also, Ashwini Mudra can be performed while sitting in a chair.

Relax the body and breathe normally.

Contract the anal sphincter muscles and breathe normally for a few seconds.

Repeat this practice for as long as you feel comfortable.

Ashwini Mudra can also be practiced in tandem with the breath. In this variation, contract the sphincter muscles while breathing in and then hold using Antah Kumbhaka (inward hold), and exhalation Bahya Kumbhaka (outward hold) where the Sphincter muscles are released. Again, your comfort level determines the length of your practice.

Kechari Mudra

Kechari Mudra (Tongue Lock) is considered the King among Mudras. In Sanskrit, the word Kha indicates Brahman or the Supreme Reality and Chara means to move. Kechari Mudra helps the practitioner to move in the blissful infinite consciousness of Brahman. Kechari is an advanced practice that enables the Yogi to reach higher states of consciousness.

Kechari Mudra is a Yoga practice where the tongue is rolled up to touch the soft palate. This is an advanced practice and the Yogi is said to overcome thirst, hunger, decay, and death by this practice.

The Kechari Mudra is done in the following manner:

Sit in a comfortable position (like those mentioned previously). Close the mouth and roll the tongue up to touch the upper palate. See how far back it can go. Initially it may touch the hard palate. Keep the tongue there for as long as comfort allows. Initially, for most practitioners, this may only last less than 1 minute. When the tongue starts to feel pain, release it and return to its normal position. Rest for some time and try again. This process can b tried even when you are engaged in light activities while sitting and walking.

The above process should be continued, and one will be able to hold the tongue on the palate for a prolonged duration.

With practice, the tongue will be able to go further back. Some day it will touch the uluva the back of the throat. With continued practice, the tongue will be able to negotiate the uluva and go behind it.

Next the tongue enters the nasal cavity. One should be able to hold there for at least a few minutes. One can breathe normally during this process. As you progress, the breathing rate will go down to 5-8 breaths per minute, or less.

Once inside the nasal cavity, the tongue can stimulate certain nerve centers that are connected to the brain. It is said that constant churning of the tongue produces a liquid that emanates from the roof of the cavity. The taste of the liquid varies. Initially, it may be salty which has to be spit out. Later, the juice turns sweet and finally Amrit (nectar) is produced and can be consumed by the Yogi which then nourishes the body.

Shambhavi Mudra—The Eyebrow Center (Bhru Madhya) Gazing Gesture

Shambhavi Mudra is a highly regarded practice in Yogic and Tantric texts. Shambhavi is a powerful Mudra used during Meditation to still the mind and to experience higher stages of consciousness. Shambhavi Mudra is mentioned in the Yogic text, Gheranda Samhita and essentially involves gazing at the eyebrow center.

Steps to Practice:

Sit in any of the Meditative Asanas mentioned previously.

The fingers can assume Jnana Mudra or Chin Mudra with the palms resting on the knees.

Shambhavi Mudra is nothing but gazing at the eyebrow center. With our eyes we cannot actually see the place where the two eyebrows meet, but an attempt is made to focus the vision between the eyebrows. Roll both eyes upwards and try to gaze at this point between the eyes.

When this is down, the practitioner will be able to see the two eyebrows as two curved lines meeting at the center. It forms a kind of V-shaped line with a dip at the center.

Concentrate the eyes on this dip in the lower center region of the V-shaped line.

Maintain this position for a long as you can. Initially the eye muscles will start to ache after a few second, or within minutes. Relax the eyes and bring them back to the normal position. Rest for a brief period and then repeat. With practice one can maintain this gaze for longer periods of time.

Breathe normally during the practice and as you continue with the Meditation technique, your breath will slow and become more subtle.

Shambhavi Mudra can take one into deeper states of Meditation.

Variations of Shambhavi Mudra

Shambhavi Mudra can also be done with eyes closed. Advanced students who have already mastered the eyebrow gazing with eyes open can attempt the same with eyes closed

Nasikagra Drishti – Nose Tip Gazing Mudra

Nasikagra Drishti or Agochari Mudra means Nose tip gazing. In Sanskrit, Nasika means the nose and agra means the tip. Drishti means sight. Thus, Nasikagra Drishti literally means gazing at the tip of the nose. Nasikagra Drishti is a powerful practice to develop concentration and is used in conjunction with Meditation techniques. Nasikagra Drishti is similar tto Sambhavi Mudra in practice, except that the eyes focus on the tip of the nose instead of the eye brow center.

Steps to Practice:

Begin in any of the comfortable Meditative poses with the spine erect. This Mudra can also be practiced by sitting on a chair if the practitioner cannot sit in an of the classic Meditation Asanas.

Keep the gaze straight and breath normally. Relax the shoulders and place the palms on your knees.

Next, slowly move your eyes and try to look at the tip of the nose. Keep the gaze there for a few seconds to begin, hold the breath to achieve further concentration, and finally release the eyes when pain or discomfort is felt.

Repeat the process as often as possible. With practice, the eyes can retain the focus on the nose tip for longer periods of time. When practicing for longer durations, one need not hold the breath. Breathing can be normal, but will usually slow down while practicing concentration. Do not strain the eyes initially, as the time will increase over months.

Additional Mudras not Discussed here:

There are pictures of these Mudras and some additional ones not discussed in the Pictorial Guide on page 90 within the Overview of Practices page.

Dhyan Murdra
Bhairav Mudra
Nasikagra Mudra
Gyan Mudra
Vishnu Mudra
Kechari Mudra
Shanmukhi Mudra
Ashwini Mudra

Chapter 14

Asanas for Meditation

General Information

Background:

Having to sit in a Meditation Posture is one reason some people shy away from Meditation since many of us simply cannot pretzel our legs into the Lotus position. However, don't let awkward looking poses and thoughts of pain keep you away from enjoying the benefits of Meditation. There are many positions we can Meditate in such as: sitting, standing, walking, and lying down. The following instructions focus on the sitting position which is the most common position for formal practices of Meditation. Sitting is conducive to staying alert and relaxed. For those unable to sit, you may use the alternate option of lying down.

Sitting Positions:

Meditation positions have one common theme and that is sitting up with a straight spine which is unsupported, and the base is firmly rooted and stable much like a tree or a mountain. The pose you assume says, "I will not be moved." The best poses are those with a wide base. This is the primary reason people are seen meditating cross-legged. But, do not allow fear of aching knees, joints, or muscles to deter you from Meditating! Over time, you may notice your flexibility improves thereby challenging you to attempt more advanced positions. All the Asanas ask is that you sit with your pelvis tilted slightly forward which accentuates the natural curve of your lower back and allows for a very strong and stable position.

The aim of the sitting posture is to balance your being upright and alert with relaxation. When exploring a sitting posture, choose a method which is relatively easy. Choosing a method that looks good, but is a significant struggle defeats the purpose of Meditation. What is most important is what you do with your mind and not what you do with your feet and legs.

Sitting in a Chair:

It is easier to stay upright and alert on a chair if you sit closer to the front edge and hold your own spine upright, instead of leaning against the backrest. If you sit with your pelvis against the back of the chair, then you could use a cushion behind your back to help keep it straight. The hips should be slightly higher than the knees which keeps you from slouching.

Keep your feet flat on the floor.
If you are much taller, or shorter than the average person, then you can compensate using a cushion under the feet if you are short, or under the buttocks if taller.

• The hands can be kept on the thighs, folded on the lap, or on top of a cushion placed on the lap.

Sitting: on a Meditation Cushion:

This is performed with your buttocks on the cushion and your legs crossed in front of you. The knees may, or may not touch the floor (depending on your flexibility). If your knees don't touch the floor, they can be supported with cushions. Over time you will become more flexible and begin to eliminate these extra supports.

Burmese position:

This pose is common in Southeast Asia. Beginners will find this position easier than Lotus, but less stable. It is a cross-legged position, but the feet remain on the floor. If your knees do not touch the floor, just relax and become accustomed to the position without forcing it (also known as Sukhasana). In time, you'll develop the flexibility needed for the Burmese and the various sitting postures such as: Swastikasana, Siddhasana, Vajrasana, Padamasana, and   Dhyan Veerasana.

Do Not attempt any Meditation positions that are uncomfortable, or too difficult for you. This prevents a clear focus on Meditation if the knees are crying out in pain. The distraction of intense agony is not acceptable! Begin with a position you can hold comfortably and gradually move into the more difficult poses. Be gentle on your knees and back. Ligaments, tendons, muscles, and joints will become more flexible over time, but you risk injury by forcing them into positions that cause pain.

Kneeling: using a Meditation Bench:

In a modified kneeling position, the buttocks are supported on a small bench which takes the body weight of the knees and feet. You can also sit kneeling with a pillow between the legs Sitting while kneeling (sitting on the feet with knees bent in front) without a bench quickly cuts off circulation to the lower legs and most people find it uncomfortable for more than a few minutes. Kneeling in the prayer position is likewise uncomfortable for more than a few minutes even with a cushion. Unless you can disengage from your physical needs for a while, you will have a hard time staying in Meditation! Avoid any kneeling positions if you have knee problems.

Lying Down: (If sitting is not an option)

The tendency to fall asleep is more of an issue, but there are ways of encouraging alertness when lying down. Place your feet comfortably apart on the floor with the knees up and not touching. If you fall asleep the knees will bump each other, or fall away causing you to wake. Another choice is keeping one of the forearms perpendicular to the floor with you elbow and upper arm resting on the floor. If sleep occurs, then the forearm will drop. Another option is holding the hands in a Mudra with the thumbs touching each other. This can work as a feedback device. When you are beginning to lose consciousness and drifting off, then the thumbs will pull apart and this should wake you bringing you back to Meditation.

Hand Position:

In all Meditation postures the hands are supposed to be positioned to support an inner current of Meditation. The recommended position is where the arms and hands can be relaxed with the palms up or down on your thighs, or folded on the lap. If there is a neck, mid-back or shoulder strain then a small cushion can be placed under the folded hands. **(See Mudras in previous section)**

Some hand positions are given below:
o   Resting in the lap with the hands facing each other and fingertips touching.
o   Resting in the lap with one hand cradled in the other.
o   Resting on top of the thighs with either palm up, or palm facing down

There are many other hand positions, but for now as you begin a consistent Meditation practice it is important to be comfortable and allow the energy to move freely in the body. Later, more advanced positions can be added, especially if you find a position which resonates with your spiritual needs.

Legs falling Asleep?

It is a common occurrence for the legs to fall asleep, as long as it doesn't take more than a minute or two for the circulation to return. As the practitioner becomes accustomed to sitting, the circulation can improve which then extends the time for them to fall asleep. For some people, different cushions such as the crescent shaped can take the pressure off and let one sit comfortably longer. It is helpful to not give in to every urge to move, but to sit with the discomfort for a while, and then slowly and mindfully make a minor adjustment to make the body more comfortable. If sitting cross-legged switching which legs are in front or on top will help

Sitting Equipment:

•   Safu: A round cushion used for sitting in Meditation usually made from cotton. A Zafu raises the hips which makes the cross-legged sitting positions more stable. It can also be used on end to place between the legs while kneeling.

- Zabuton: A square or rectangular padded mat that can sit under the Zafu, or bench to cushion the knees and ankles which is helpful on hard floors. Seiza Bench: A wooden bench used in the kneeling posture which raises the buttocks so as not to compress the legs.

General Guidance:

Students are advised to keep the following approach in mind while practicing Hatha Yogasanas to prepare their mind-body for Meditative postures:

The goal of practice is not to perfect the external form of the postures. Postures are viewed as tools to release chronic tension, stretch and strengthen the body, and increase self-awareness. Postures can be modified to meet individual needs.

With regular practice one becomes more sensitive to the needs of their body and are naturally drawn to make healthier choices about diet, exercise, and other lifestyle habits.

Develop an emphasis on being present in the body by sustaining flowing breath
o   Learning to listen to the body and honor its needs.
Discover the same principles that bring out the best in you on the Yoga mat can be applied to daily life. Learn how to meet the challenges with a sense of relaxation, self-acceptance, strength, courage, and openness to change.

Regular practice stimulates an ongoing process of positive change which inspires you to realize your full potential.

The overall experience is one of learning to love and nurture the body and not whip it into shape.

Acknowledge that regular practice is designed to initiate a process of personal transformation.

Practical Applications:

Wear loose clothing and if necessary, the belt should not be tightened.

The mouth is kept closed, unless you have some type of nasal blockage, and breathing is through the nose.

The tongue can be pressed lightly against the upper palate. This may reduce the need to salivate and swallow.

In our tradition we recommend the eyes remain shut, but it is permitted to Meditate with the eyes open if necessary. Usually, this is done with the eyes lowered, gaze resting on the ground about two or three feet in front of the practitioner.

The chin is slightly tucked in.

Chapter 15

Meditative Asanas – (Practical Applications)

Sukhasana (The Easy Sitting Pose)

Sukhasana, or the easy sitting pose, is one of the simplest poses for Meditation suited for all beginners. Sukhasana comes from the Sanskrit word "Sukham which can mean comfort, easy, joyful, pleasure, etc. Sukhasana can be done by all age groups. This Asana is the simplest of the sitting postures in Yoga, is easy to perform, and can be done even by elderly people. But, those with serious knee or hip injuries should avoid this posture.

Steps to Practice:

Sit on the floor with legs stretched out. Always us a Yoga mat, cushion, or carpet while sitting on the floor.

Fold the left leg and tuck it inside the right thigh.

Next fold the right leg and tuck it inside the left thigh.

Keep the hands on the knees. Jnana/Chin Mudra can be used of you are using this posture for Meditation

Sit erect with the spine straight.

Relax you whole body and breathe normally.

Maintain this position for as long as you are comfortable.

Swastikasana – The Auspicious Pose

Swastikasana, or the Auspicious Pose is an easy Meditation pose for those who cannot attempt the more difficult Asanas like Padamasana and Siddhasana. The India symbol of the Swastika is a symbol of auspiciousness. In Swastikasana, the position of the legs resemble the symbol of the Swastika which comes from the Sanskrit rood words – Su meaning good Asti meaning to be, or existence, and Ka meaning to make. This Asana can be described as one that helps to realize the unity of existence. Swastikasana is relatively easy to perform and can be used for Meditative purposes and for prolonged sitting.

Steps to Practice:

Sit on the floor with legs spread out in front of you.

Fold the left leg and place the sole of the left leg against the inner thigh of the right leg.

Bend the right leg and place the right foot in the space between the left thigh and calf muscles.

Grasp the left foot by the toes and pull it up and place it between the right calf and thigh.

The knees should firmly touch the floor.

Adjust the pose so that you feel comfortable

Keep the body and trunk straight

Siddhasana (The Accomplished Pose)

In Hatha Yoga Pradeepika, it is said that a Yoga practitioner should always practice Siddhasana from among the 84 Asanas. The text says that practice of Siddhasana purifies all the 72,000 nadis, or energy channels in the body through which the Prana flows. This Asana can be practiced by anyone, except those suffering from sciatica, or sacral infections.

Steps to Practice:

Sit on the floor with the legs close to each other.

Take the left food and place it at the perineum. The perineum is the soft tissue between the anus and the testis for males. For females, should place the left foot in the labia majora of the vagina

Now take the right foot and place it over the left foot.

To make the posture steadier, slide the toes of the right foot into the space between the left calf muscles. This may require some adjustment to the position as it creates a lock, so the lower body is stable for longer durations of Meditation.

The knees should touch the floor. Insure the spin is straight and maintain this position as long as you are comfortable

Vajrasana (The Thunderbolt Pose)

Vajrasana, or the kneeling Yoga pose is also called the Diamond pose, or the Thunderbolt pose. The name comes from the Sanskrit word Vajra which can mean Thunderbolt or Diamond. Normally, Asanas should be performed on an empty stomach, but Vajrasana is one of the few exceptions. This Asana can be done immediately after the meal and in fact, is most effective after the meal which aids in digestion.

Steps to Practice:

Rest on the knees with the lower legs together and stretched backwards with the two big toes crossing each other.

Lower your body and sit on you heels with the buttocks resting on the heels, and the thighs on the calf muscles.

72

Keep your hands on your knees and keep the head straight. Concentrate on the breath and observe the process of inhalation and exhalation.One may close the eyes to get an excellent concentration and for calming the mind.

Remain in this position for at least 5-10 minutes. In the initial stages there may be pain in the legs when you sit in this position. When this occurs undo the Asana and stretch the legs. Massage the ankles, knees, and calf muscles with the hands. With practice one can rest in this position in this position.

Do not do this Asana if you have knee problems, or if you have had recent surgeries as it may put additional strain on the knees. Also, pregnant women should try this Asana with their knees apart to avoid stress on the abdomen.

Padamasana (The Lotus Pose):

Padamasana is considered one of the best poses for Meditation. In Padamasana, the legs are locked together, and the lower body is absolutely stable. Also, the back and spine will be straight. This is perfect for longer periods of Meditation as the body can be held motionless with the least distractions. People suffering from sciatica and sacral pain, weak knee joints, etc. should avoid this Asana.

Ardh Padamasana

Padamasana

Steps to Practice:

Sit on the floor comfortably. Assume the simple cross-legged pose where the legs are folded.

Lift the left leg and place it on the right thigh. Now, lift the right leg and place it over the left leg. The knees must touch the floor, but if they don't, do not worry. With practice this will happen once the legs become flexible.

Pull and adjust the legs so the soles of the feet face upwards and the heels are then tucked in at the waist near the pelvic bone.

Next, make the spine straight, broaden the chest (to avoid stooping), and place the hands in the gap between the feet. Place the left palm over the right palm. Relax the muscles in the abdomen and chest. The shoulders should be absolutely relaxed.

You may close the eyes and breathe slowly and deeply. Let the awareness be on the breathing process as you experience the perfect balance and alignment of the entire body.

Maintain this position for as long as comfortable. Those who wish to use this pose for Meditation should sit for at least 20 minutes. Slowly increase the time so that your duration of Meditation can also increase. At some point, the legs may start to ache. Once you have crossed your threshold of pain, slowly release the legs and massage them gently until the pain is gone. Over a period of time you will be able to sit for longer durations in this Asana. Those who are young will master this Asana quickly. After the age of 30-35 years of age the body is less supple. Of course, with practice anyone, even those above 60 years of age can master this Asana. It is said that if one can sit in an Asana for three and a half hours, then one is said to have attained Siddhi (spiritual/magical capability) in that Asana. One need not go to such extremes, even 30 minutes to an hour is good enough for most practitioners.

One of the main points to be noted in Meditative Asanas is that the body should be absolutely still and relaxed. There should be no pain or stress, otherwise instead of Meditating, the attention will be drawn to the body and its discomforts. One may use a soft support (pillow, cushion) under the buttocks to achieve comfort.

Padamasana can also be done with left leg over the right leg. In this case, first place the right leg on the left thigh. Then the left leg is placed over the right leg. However, traditionally it is practiced the other way (with the right leg over left).

Padamasana is not easy for beginners. In such cases, some joint exercises will be required to bring about flexibility. One can do any exercise that stretches the lower legs, thighs, and waist muscles to get this flexibility and should try first Ardh

Padamasana (Half-Lotus pose) where one foot is on the top of the opposite thigh (as in full Lotus) and one is under the opposite thigh. This position is nearly as stable as in Full Lotus. If you use the half Lotus, switch out which leg is on top to avoid achieving flexibility on only one side.

Makarasana (Crocodile Pose)

Makarasana, or the Crocodile pose is a Yoga Asana used for relaxation. In Sanskrit, Makar means Crocodile, and Asana means pose. Makarasana is a Yogic pose useful for people with back and shoulder problems.

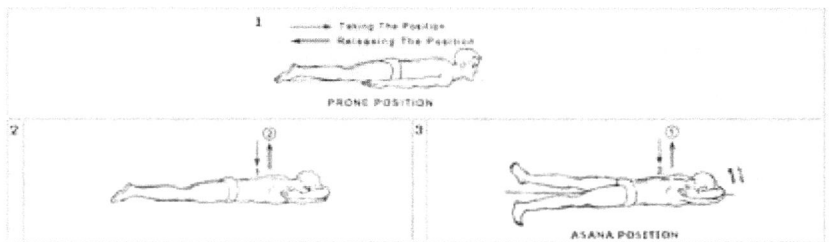

Steps to Practice:

Lie down on the floor on your stomach with your hands folded under the head. Place the palms on your shoulders in a relaxed way and close the eyes. Stretch the legs as far as possible. The toes should point outwards. Relax the whole body. Breathe normally and slowly as you feel the entire body touching the ground and the deep relaxation in all your muscles. Relax in this posture for 2-5 minutes.

Alternate Method:

Lie down on your chest with the head on the floor. Place the elbows on the ground and raise your head and shoulders. Then rest the head in the palms of the hands The legs should be kept straight and relaxed, then close the eyes. Remain in this position for 2-5 minutes.

Shavasana (Corpse Pose):

Shavasana, the corpse pose is a Yogic relaxation pose. The name comes from the Sanskrit words Shava meaning corpse and Asana meaning posture. Shavasana is the simplest and the main relaxation pose used in Yoga. It is usually performed at the beginning and at the end of Yoga practice. It is also used as a resting pose between other Yoga Asanas.

76

In Shavasana, emphasis is given to slow, rhythmic and relaxed breathing. The Yogic breath is a complete breath done with full awareness. The abdomen, the chest, and the neck (clavicular region) expand during a relaxed deep breath. As one relaxes more, the abdominal breathing is more prominent. We may have the habit of breathing from the chest and neck regions when we are tense. One may observe that when we are relaxed, the abdominal breathing takes over. A great example is to observe the breathing of an infant lying on its back in bed. Notice how slowly and rhythmically the child breathes and how smoothly the abdomen goes up and down. Observe the up and down motion of t he abdomen. This relaxed breathing comes naturally to children when they are born, but as the body ages irregularities develop in the breathing process due to the stress and strains of living. Also, women tend to use clavicular breathing (or breathing from the neck region) during pregnancy as it is difficult to do full abdominal breathing during that stage. This is normal, but what happens is that for many women this may become a habit even after the delivery of the child.

All these problems with irregular breathing can be corrected by practicing Yogic breath. In Yogic breath as one inhales and expands the abdomen first, then the chest, and ends with the neck. When breathing out the process is reversed where the neck and chest regions contract first and then ends at the abdomen.

Steps to Practice:

- Lie down on the floor on your back. Place your hands next to the body and slightly spread out with the palms facing upwards. Spread the legs at a slight angle and feel as relaxed as possible. Consciously relax all the muscles in the body from head to toe. Allow the breathing to be slow and deep while focusing the attention on the belly and observe the slow and rhythmic abdominal breathing.
- Maintain this position for as long as needed ranging from 5-30 minutes and try not to sleep during the process. To release this position, take a few deep breaths and slowly roll over to one side, then use the arms and raise to the seated position.

Vipareeta Karani Asana (Inverted Pose)

Vipareeta Karana Asana or the inverted pose comes from the Sanskrit word Vipareeta meaning Inverted and Karani meaning doing. Vipareeta Karani Asana is one of the simplest of the inverted Asanas and hence easy to perform. Those who have difficulty doing the difficult inverted poses like Sirsana (head stand) and Sarvangasana (shoulder stand) can get similar benefits by doing Vipareeta Karani Asana. This asana is all the basic pose for the Vipareeta Karani Mudra.

Inverted Asanas like Vipareeta Karani Asana have a special effect on the human body. Usually, all the organs are pulled downwards due to the gravitational force. While performing inverted Asanas one is trying to reverse this effect. This can have various health benefits, especially for those suffering from piles and hydrocele.

However, it is good to consult a qualified Yoga instructor and your doctor before attempting inverted Asanas for therapeutic reasons. If you suffer from the following, please consult with your doctor before beginning Inverted poses.
o   **High blood pressure**
o   **Bad neck conditions**
o   **Heart problems**
o   **Inflammation of the spleen or liver**

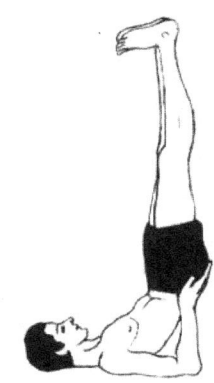

Steps to Practice:

Begin with the supine position by lying on your back in a relaxed way. Let the hands rest on the floor next to the body and breathe normal.

Try to raise the legs slowly till they are almost 90 degrees to the floor. Now, place the hands under the lower back at the waist level. Use the hands and elbows for support to raise your body up further.

The breath should be held inside when you are raising the body to the vertical position.
Use the support of the hands to raise the trunk further up until the whole trunk is about 45 degrees to the ground and the legs are vertical. At this stage, the body weight rests on the shoulders. Hand and elbows remain as props to support and balance the body.

In the final pose, the legs are 90 degrees to the floor and the trunk is about 45 degrees to the floor.

Remain in this position according to our own comfort level. For health benefits 3-5 minutes per day is sufficient, but practitioners can remain in position for up to 15 minutes to enhance the Spiritual benefits.

Breathe normally while maintaining the steady raised position.

While releasing the position, the breath is held inside, and the body is slowly brought down to the supine position.

After performing Vipareeta Karani Asana, usually a counter Asana like Matsyasana, Ushtrasana, or Supta Vajrasana is performed for half the duration.

Chapter 16

Meditations

Breathing Meditation:

This Meditation is very good for not only breathing, but can assist with mental, or physically based depressions. If done prior to Meditating, you will find a difference in the quality of your Meditation. It would benefit the practitioner to practice this exercise for a long time and seek perfection. Train your body to follow your mental instructions and you will find a difference in the quality of your sleep as it also increases the duration of the sleep periods. Do not retain breath in this exercise and avoid jerks, noises, and shallow breathing.

Steps to Practice

- Lie down on your back with legs slightly apart, arms at your sides with palms up, and eyes half-open, or closed.
- Focus on the breath and how the air moves in and out of the body.
- Take several deep breaths and as you begin to feel comfortable and relaxed, return to normal breathing.
- Exhale from Crown to Perineum, and inhale from Perineum to the Crown 10 repetitions.
- Do the same between Eye-brow center to Heart center, throat, and bridge of the nostrils.
- Then allow the breath to flash at the eyebrow center like a candle flame.
- Reverse the process coming back to the Crown and Perineum.

Hasya (Laughter) Yoga

Hasya (Laughter) Yoga is the practice of laughter as a form of exercise which is free from the need of jokes, or comedy where Yogic Postures and Breathing are integrated with intentional laughter techniques that are simple, gentle, and easier to practice in a group with lots of fun.

Modern society the world over is now realizing the importance of Laughter considered to be one of the inherent characteristics of human behavior as a therapy. This was due to an awareness of the suffering of the multitudes from the effects of chronic stress, tension, and anxiety. Yoga, when combined with Laughter evolves a healing system which can give amazing results for diseases as well as being a preventative measure.

Basic rules for Hasya Yoga

Clap in rhythm while chanting Ho - Ho - Ha – Ha This is different from regular clapping. The clapping is performed with hands in full contact with each other, swinging the hands back and forth from left to right. Smile while chanting Ho Ho Ha Ha maintaining eye contact with those next to you. This warm up exercise and stimulates acupressure points on the palms, improves blood circulation in the entire body, and aids in bringing about a sense of well-being while building energy levels.

Breathing: Inhale for as long as you lift the arms up (height of the arms does not matter) and exhale for as long as the arms are going down (be sure to bend forward in this exercise during exhalation to release lower tension). The pace is up to the practitioner where movement can be fast or slow; small and large. Breath can be through the mouth, or nose. The goal is to consciously deepen the breath while staying within a comfortable range of motion. Breathing through the nose or mouth is unimportant at this stage and comfort for the practitioner is the highest concern.

Appreciation Gesture: Join your pointing finger with the thumb to make a small circle and make a gesture as if you are appreciating the group members while saying, "Very Good, Very Good, Very Good," and laughing simultaneously.

Laugh: The last part of this process is critical, and you are urged to laugh as often and as loud as possible. This is, of course, the best part and you are urged to do the following:

Maintain eye contact! This is very important as it helps to keep the mind in the here and now plus laughter is visually contagious.

Please refrain from Speaking! No jokes pleas. Talking and joking sabotages your own laughter potential so please let your joy flow freely.Fake is Okay! Whether you genuinely laugh or not, it makes very little difference. Either way you will breathe a lot and benefit from the exercise. Act happy and energetic. A joyful spirit is noisy, so move around, smile, interact with others, and act happy! Be energetic and let the group hear you! Acting this way will make you feel joyful.

How to Practice:

Template Laughter Session (Duration 20-30 minutes minimum)

Step 1 – Clapping in a rhythm 1-2, 1-2-3 accompanied with chanting of Ho-Ho-Ha-Ha-Ha

Step 2 – Practice Laughter Exercises (each exercise must end saying, "Very Good," (three times) and chanting Ho-Ho-Ha-Ha-Ha a few times.

Greeting Laughter: joining both the hands and greeting in Indian style (Namaste) or shanking hands (Western Style) with at leas 4-5 people in the group and laugh

Milk Shake Laughter (variation): Hold and mix two imaginary glasses of milk or coffee and at the instruction of the leader pour the milk from one glass into the other by chanting Aeee…, and then pour it back into the first glass by chanting Aeee…, After that, everyone laughs making a gesture as if they are drinking milk. (Repeat 4 times)

Swinging Laughter: Stand in a circle and move towards the center by chanting Hee…and Ha Ha Ha while away from the center.

Lion Laughter: Extend the tongue fully with eyes wide open and hands stretched out like the claws of a lion and laugh from the stomach.

Motorboat (or lawnmower) laughter: Lets start an old gas engine lawnmower. Put one foot on the machine to hold it still and grab the pull cord. We are going to pull and crank it in 4 powerful laughs. Move around and keep laughing once your engine is started. Ready? Go! Ha -Ha Ha – Ha Ha Ha – Ha ha ha ha ha ha ha

Some thoughts on Laughter Meditation:

It is the most pleasurable part of the laughter session. By now the diaphragm (muscle used when laughing) has been stimulated and begins to take a life of its own. Sit down (floor is best, on a chair is acceptable) and begin by spending a few seconds to minutes in complete silence and stillness.

By sitting down the diaphragm gets freed from muscular restrictions by surrounding muscles. This in turn opens the door for its full expression. Free-flow, uproarious, belly-rippling laughter (all for no reason whatsoever) is right behind the corner.

Warning: Laughter Yoga is not a substitute for proper medical consultation for any physical, mental, or psychological illnesses and may not be suitable for everyone. It is contra-indicated for people suffering from uncontrolled high blood pressure, heart disease, epilepsy, hernia issues, sever backaches, and any major psychiatric disorders. This list is for guidance only and is not meant to be exhaustive. If in doubt do not try this meditation and consult your trained medical professional for guidance.

Japa-Ajapa Meditation

Japa means repeating, or remembering the Mantra, and Ajapa-Japa means constant awareness. The letter A in front of the word Japa means without. Thus, Ajapa-Japa is the practice of Japa without the mental effort normally needed to repeat the Mantra. In other words, it has begun to come naturally, thereby turning into a constant awareness. The practice of constant remembrance evolves in stages.

Steps to Practice:

At first, intentionally repeat the syllables of the Mantra internally, as if you are talking to yourself in your mind. Then, allow the inner sound to come at whatever speed feels comfortable to the mind. Sometimes it is very slow, as if the mind were wading through a vat of honey. At other times, it is very rapid, as if flying through the sky without restraint.

With practice, the Mantra Japa is repeated automatically, like a song that you have heard many times, which just comes on its own.

Gradually the practitioner remembers the Mantra with attention drawn to it. It is more like noticing what is already happening, rather than causing it to happen. This is somewhat like the attention stance of listening rather than speaking though you might not literally hear the sound.

In time, the feeling of the Mantra is there even when the sound, or remembering of the syllables is not there. When the syllables fade away, the feeling may still be there. This is remembrance of the feeling of the Mantra.

As the practice evolves, there comes a pervasive awareness of the Mantra, which is subtler than both the syllables and any surface level meaning or definition. This constant awareness is the meaning of Ajapa-Japa

Mala Mantra Meditation

Japa Mala or Mala Beads have been used by our Great Masters from time immemorial. Traditionally, A Guru (Master) gives the Mala to his disciple along with a Mantra to initiate him into a spiritual path.

In modern times, Mala has become an essential accessory in Meditation practice. Many people wear Malas used for Meditation as ornaments as more of a fashion statement and to show off their spiritual associations without knowing the spiritual importance of a Mala. The following will uncover the symbolism and the significance of a Mala from a Meditation perspective.

What is a Mala?

In Sanskrit language, Mala or more correctly Maala means a garland of beads. Malas used for counting the affirmations, or Mantra repetitions of Meditation are called Japa Mala, or just Mala. The process of repeating a Mantra or a phrase is called Japa.

Why 108 beads?

Generally, a Hindu Japa Mala consists of 108 + 1 beads with a knot between the beads. The number 108 has several meanings. Some of them are:

- 27 constellations x 4 padas (parts)   = 108
- 12 Zodiac houses x 9 planets   = 108
- Upanishads (Scriptures of the Vedas)   = 108

In other words, 108 beads represent the entire universe. When we count the Mantra using the Mala, we are remembering the presence of the Deity who is the Universal Self in every part of the universe. So, after each cycle of repetition, we cover the entire universe by feeling and touching the presence of the deity and the Mantra in it. 108 beads symbolize the universe and repeating each one reminds us of the omnipresence of the Universal Self. It suggests the immanent nature of the Universal self.

The Guru: 109th Bead of Mala

There is an additional 109th bead knotted in the Mala referred to as Sumeru, Meru bead, Guru bead, etc. To show respect to a Guru (master) the Guru bead is never crossed when counting the Mantras during Meditation. Instead, the Mala is turned around so that the next round of counting begins with the 108th bead. The Guru bead is separate from the main Mala. As discussed earlier, the 108 beads of the Mala make up the universe suggesting the Universal Self is transcendental, i.e. beyond the universe.

The Guru bead is the 109th bead making it separate from the universe of 108 beads which means it is a force beyond the universe and becomes the Universal Self. This can also mean that Guru is nothing but God. The tassel after the Guru bead indicates the fourth state called Turiya.

The four states of consciousness are Jagrat, Svapna, Shushupti, and Turiya. Jagrat is waking consciousness, Svapna is the dream consciousness, Shushupti is the deep sleep consciousness and Turiya is higher consciousness which is beyond all previous states.

The String of the Mala symbolizes the Universal Self. This can be seen by considering how the beads form the part of the universe and the string holds and supports the beads, therefore the string symbolizes the Universal Self which is the force supporting and sustaining every part and every being of the universe.

The Circular arrangement of beads: In a Japa Mala, 108 beads are strung in a circular fashion. It represents the cyclic nature of the universe without an end or a beginning. The Universal Self is the only unchanging principle, much like a string in the Mala. The circular arrangement also signifies the Infinite cycle of birth and death. Therefore, the highest goal of our lives is to permanently escape from this cycle by merging with the Universal Self. The beads are like different births or bodies. By contemplating the Mantra of the deity continuously, we would like to access the inherent thread of the universe (the Universal Self) which is eternal and unchanging.

Knot between the beads: Traditionally, a knot is kept between the beads to ensure that the beads won't touch each other. This is to avoid the distraction that may be caused due to frictional sounds of beads during Mantra Meditation. A knot signifies the divine link present between all beings of this universe.

Mantra Meditation:

Chanting Mantras is an ancient Meditation technique extensively used in Tibet and India. A Mantra is intrinsically related to sound; Mantras are sound, and sound reverberates in all things in the universe. Within human beings there is a self-born and indestructible sound which repeats itself constantly. Sound has enormous power, and if fact, has the power to create an entire universe. According to ancient Indian Vedic texts, in the beginning there was sound which reverberated as Om and from that sound everything came into existence. God originally manifested as sound. In order to Meditate on Mantra Meditation, use the steps below.

Steps to Practice:

Sit comfortably in a Meditative pose in a quiet place. Close the eyes and begin chanting the Mantra (loud, whisper, silent)

Repeat the Mantra with faith and respect. Repeat with full awareness of its meaning.

Keep chanting the Mantra for 20 minutes. (Use a timer for keeping track of time) After 20 minutes stop chanting, be quiet, and sit silently.

The Mantra will keep echoing in your mind for some time. Be watchful of what occurs inside of you. Don't judge, act, or react. Be aware of all that is happening inside of you. Be a witness of all your emotions, feelings, and other activities in and around you. You will feel a sense of calm and bliss. All thought activities will start decreasing and eventually come to a standstill. Slowly open your eyes and move out of the Meditation.

Mindfulness Meditation

Mindfulness is the practice of purposely focusing your attention on the present moment and accepting it without judgement. Mindfulness is now being examined scientifically and has been found to be a key element in happiness. Practicing Mindfulness can bring improvements in both physical and psychological symptoms as well as positive changes in heal attitudes and behaviors.

Steps to Practice:

Sit straight on a chair or cross-legged position on the floor.

Focus on your breathing; sensations of air flowing into the nostrils, out the mouth, and the stomach rising and falling from inhalation/exhalation.

Body Sensations: Notice subtle body sensation if there are any such as itching, or tingling without judgement and allow them to pass.

Sensory: Notice sights, sounds, smells, tastes, and touch and then name them accordingly to the sense they represent, again without passing judgment and then releasing them.

85

Emotions: Allow emotions to be present without judgment. Practice a steady and relaxed naming of emotions such as joy, anger, frustration, etc. Accept the presence of these emotions without judgement and allow them to pass.

Urge surfing: Cope with cravings (for addictive substances or behaviors) and allow them to pass. Notice how your body feels as the craving enters.

Embrace and consider each though, sensation, or urge without judgement regardless if good or bad. If the mind begins to wander, return your focus to your breathing, then expand your awareness once more.

Nada Yoga Meditation

Nada Yoga uses sound and music as a medium to penetrate the layers of the mind and believes the body and mind are solidifications of the sound. This is an excellent practice for inducing Pratyahara (disassociation of the mind from the surroundings and senses. In Yoga there are Anahata (Internal) and Ahata (external) sounds. Through the practice of Nada Yoga, the practitioner can become sensitive to the inner sounds of the body.

Steps to Practice:

Sit in any Meditative Asana with eyes close. Keep your spine straight in a relaxed manner. Breathe in slowly, easily,,deeply and then breathe out in the same manner.

Start Bhramari Pranayama with humming bee sound for 10 minutes.

Next, be silent and wait, as you listen Anahata Nada. From the Sanskrit Anahata means unstuck/unbeaten and Nada means to flow and can be thought of as the unmade sound which is omnipresent and all pervasive; present in the absence of anything to create noise.

Focus on the silence in between two sounds for 10 minutes.

Bring your attention to your inner sounds (Anahata Nada) There is absolutely no need to put pressure on yourself. Be relaxed, simply listen, and enjoy the process. For a sample Nada Yoga Meditation session see page 105.

Osho Nataraj Meditation

Nataraj is the energy of dance which becomes a total Meditation where all inner division disappear, and a subtle and relaxed awareness remains.

"Forget the dance; the center of the ego and become the dance. This is the Meditation. Dance so deeply you forget completely you are dancing and begin to feel you are the dance. The division must disappear and then it becomes a Meditation. If the division is there, then it is an exercise which is good and healthy, but it cannot be said to be spiritual. It is just a simple dance. Dance is good in itself-, and as far as it goes it is good. After it, you will feel fresh and young, but it is not Meditation yet. The dance must go, until only the dance remains. Don't stand aside; don't be an observer. Participate! Be playful! Remember the word playful always – with me it is very basic." Osho

Steps to Practice:

First Stage: 40 minutes
With eyes closed dance if possessed. Let your unconscious take over completely. Do not control your movements or witness what is happening. Just be totally in the dance

Second Stage: 20 minutes
Keeping the eyes closed lie down immediately. Be silent and still.

Third Stage: 5 minutes
Dance in celebration and enjoy!

Osho Kundalini Meditation

The best time for Kundalini Meditation is in the evening after work, school, or may be simply even if you have been idle. There are 4 stages in Kundalini Meditation with each stage comprising 15 minutes and music played in the background.

Stage 1: 15 minutes

In the first stage as the music begins simply loosen yourself and allow the shaking to happen with it beginning in the legs. Initially, even if the shaking doesn't happen don't worry. Allow things to happen as they are happening. Once you feel the shaking in your leg start, then gradually allow the movement from your legs move to the other parts of your body. Begin to observe yourself, your thoughts, and the inner-self.

Stage 2: 15 minutes

Dance, rejoice, and move the body the way you want to and celebrate. Yes, move your body any way you desire and do not refrain, feel shy, and remember this is not a dance competition. If you are in a group, don't bother about any other person around you and simply remain centered towards yourself as you enjoy the experience.

Stage 3: 15 minutes

In the third stage either stand the way you stopped after your dance, or gently sit down in a relaxing position. With the music playing close the eyes and start observing your thoughts coming from the mind. Do not focus on whether they are good or bad, but instead let them come without any judgement or guilt. Watch them internally with a neutral attitude.

Stage 4: 15 minutes

In the fourth stage there is no music and only silence. This period ends with the sounds of a song. Lie down and continue to observe your thoughts and your inner sky. Allow yourself to relax, relax, relax.

Pulse Meditation

Meditation can be as simple as finding your pulse. It improves your concentration and brings calm to even the most scattered mind. You can find your pulse on the Wrist, Navel, Throat, and Crown Chakra.

Steps to Practice:

Sit comfortable cross-legged on the floor. The hand position – Place the four fingers of your right hand on the left wrist and feel the pulse. The fingers are in a straight line with them lightly pressing on the wrist to allow you to feel the pulse in each fingertip. (10 minutes)

Now lie down in Shavasana and keep the body steady and relaxed completely. Put all your fingertips on the navel and press a little. You will feel a pulsation there. Maintain your attention there for: (10 minutes).

Use the same method to find the pulse at the throat. To feel a **pulse** on the side of the **neck** just below the jaw line, place your index and middle fingers in the hollow between the windpipe and the large muscle in the **neck**. Press lightly until you feel a **pulse**. (10 minutes)

To find the pulse at the Crown Chakra, use the same fingers and lightly press against the scalp in the center of the Crown. (10 minutes)

This meditation can be done anytime, and place, and you can experience great benefits in just one minute. Practice this daily to develop your intuition and calm the mind. You can also Meditate on the Navel pulse, pulse on the throat, or Crown Chakra as well.

Relaxation Meditation

Relaxation Meditation is the technique that gives you an opportunity to let go, relax, and Meditate. It has the potential of activating the body's natural defenses to heal and harmonize all the Kosha and should not be practiced more than 20 minutes. One should not fall asleep during this Meditation.

Steps to Practice:

Lie down in Shavasana on the back, legs and feet slightly apart, with the arms at the side of the body and eyes closed. Begin Puraka (inhalation) and Rechaka (exhalation) slowly and evenly. First relax the limbs physically and then as the mind to travel with a feeling of relaxation.

Start by relaxing the forehead, facial muscles, neck, shoulders continuing in a downward motion until the toes are reached.

Then, begin the journey upwards from toes to head while you continue to relax each set of muscles.

Now, inhale and create voluntary tension in the right leg. Maintain the state of tension for at least 10 seconds and then release. Relax and let go of the tension in the leg.

Repeat the same with the left leg, moving to the chest, abdomen, arms, and face.

Next, let your body be loose and relaxed completely without any voluntary movement.

Now, turn your awareness to the breath and notice each inhalation and exhalation. Let the breath flow without pauses, jerks, or noise.

Take your awareness to each part of the body and Meditate on that part of the body. At this stage, using the body's 61 energy points begin with #1 at the forehead, and then end with number 61 at the center of the forehead. Finally, feel a sense of complete relaxation.

Satnaam Kirtan

Kirtan Kriya is a Meditation chant exercise originating from Kundalini Yoga involving a combination of chanting and using Mudras (finger poses). This simple Meditative exercise reduces stress levels, increases circulation in the brain, promotes focus and clarity, and finally, stimulates the mind-body-spirit connection. The four Sanskrit chanting sounds used in this Meditation (SA TA NA MA) translates to: birth, life, death, rebirth. You can practice Kirtan Kriya for as little as 10-12 minutes each day.

Steps to Practice:

Begin your session by sitting cross-legged on the floor, or seated upright in a straight-backed chair. Rest your hands on your knees with palms facing upwards.

Chant the syllables, Sa, Ta, Na, Ma – lengthen the ending of each sound as you repeat them...aaaaaaah

Touch your index finger tip to the tip of your thumb as you chant Sa(aaaah)
Touch your middle finger tip to the tip of your thumb as you chant Ta(aaaah)
Touch your ring finger tip to the tip of your thumb as you chant Na(aaaaah)
Touch your pinky tip to the tip of your thumb as you chant Ma(aaaaah)

Perform the finger movements shown above as you chant in the following sequence:

Chant out loud for 5 minutes.

Chant in a whisper for 5 minutes

Chant in silence for 10 minutes.

Chant in a whisper for 2 minutes

Chant out loud for 2 minutes.

Sahaj Yog Dhyan

Shri Mataji Nirmala Devi was born on the March 21, 1923 in India and died on 23 February 2011 in Genoa, Italy. She is the founder of Sahaja Yoga, a Meditation technique discovered in 1970.

There is an innate spiritual potential within every human being which can be spontaneously awakened through the unique process of Sahaja Yoga. This awakening can be described as self-realization.

The inner balance and stress reduction that accompanies the practice of Sahaja Yoga Meditation has already benefited hundreds of thousands worldwide. With practice individuals are able to direct their own energy and redress mental, physical, and emotional imbalances to achieve a state of well-being, serenity and fulfillment.

Steps to Practice:

Sit comfortably with the palm of the left hand facing upwards on your lap. Use the right hand as indicated on the left side of the body to support the movement of the Kundalini upwards. You can use the affirmations silently repeating them inside without speaking them outside. Please use the affirmations with all your confidence and pure desire to become the Spirit. Each of the steps shown below will be repeated 7 times except for Step 6 which is repeated 16 times.

Step 1:

Place your right hand over your heart and ask the following question to yourself:

Mother, Am I the Spirit?

Step 2:

Move the right hand to the lower left part of the sternum (last 2 ribs) and ask the following question:

Mother, Am I my own Master?

Step 3:

 Move the right hand lower to the stomach area and request the following:
Mother, please give me Pure Knowledge.

Step 4:

After this request, raise the hand once more to the sternum area shown in Step 2 and assert the following:

Mother, I am my own Master!

Step 5:

Move the right hand upwards to the Heart and assert the following:

Mother, I am the Spirit!

Step 6:

Take the right hand and place it at the side of the neck, turn the face to the right and repeat the Affirmation 16 times:

Mother, I am not guilty at all.

Step 7:

Move the right hand to the Forehead and repeat the following affirmation:

Mother, I forgive everyone, everything, and especially forgive myself.

Step 8:

Move the right hand to the back of the head and repeat the following:

If I have done any wrong against the Param Chaithanya and its powers, please forgive me.

Step 9:

Move the right hand to the top of the head at the fontanel area, rotate your scalp in a clockwise direction seven times. In each time pray the following with humbleness:

Mother, please give me Self-Realization.

Satsang Meditation

SATSANG is a combination of two words: SAT means truth and SANG means company. The company of the true one's is SATSANG.

SATSANG can be done in the company of a Guru (Master), the company of good people, or even alone in the company of one's soul (the highest truth). This meditation can be of various forms like reading scriptures, discussing about truth, Meditating, grasping good qualities of others, and listening to the Guru.

SATSANG can be called the first step towards enlightenment because the first lesson in a spiritual journey is understanding by listening to more divine and experienced people.

The most common form of SATSANG is listening to a divine personality who has achieved a level of excellence. The first step for beginners of a spiritual life is SATSANG because beginners usually are of a lower consciousness, and if they start reading a book it will go over their head and possibly misunderstood.

When in a SATSANG everything is placed in front of you as a practical

SATSANG in the company of learned men gives great inspiration to a beginner when they see a person who posses great spiritual excellence which would make them want to achieve the same in their lives. SATSANG is mostly done in the presence of many people. A feeling of a group and guidance of a learned Guru will help immensely in your spiritual path.

Self-Inquiry Meditation

True self-inquiry is not just questioning the limitations of our outer identity like: Family affiliation (wife, father, sister, brother, etc.), or religious affiliation (Christian, Catholic, Hindu, Atheist, etc.)

Self-inquiry, moreover, is not merely an intellectual or psychological inquiry, but one that probes one's entire energy and attention. It requires a full and one-sided concentration which is not interrupted by the intrusion of other thoughts.

Self-inquiry means to constantly question and reverse this process of extroversion by seeking out the origin of our awareness and energy in the heart. It directs us back to the pure "I" that is not identified with any form of objectivity, physical or mental.

The true self is not only beyond human distinction, but is beyond all divisions of time and space, name and form, birth and death. It is beyond all experience.

Self-inquiry leads us ultimately to the Absolute in which the phenomenal world becomes little more than a mirage of the mind and senses. It goes far beyond the discovery of some greater self, or any human or creative potential and to what is beyond all limitations.

Steps to Practice:

Ask yourself "Who Am I? and Say to Yourself the following:

I am not the body.

I am not the mind

I am not the intellect or Ego

I am neither Panch Prana nor Panch Kosha

I am not affected by the merit of pain or pleasure, heat or cold.

I am not enjoyment; the thing being enjoyed or the person enjoying

I have no Father or Mother, nor do I have any brothers, friends, Guru, or Shishya (relationship & knowledge gained between Guru/Student) I am that which has no birth and no death. I am the auspicious, blissful, unconditioned consciousness.

Transcendental Meditation

The Transcendental Meditation technique is a specific form of Mantra Meditation developed by Mararishi Mahesh Yogi and is often referred to as TM. This Meditation practice involves the use of a Mantra and is practiced for 15-20 minutes twice per day while sitting with one's eyes closed. TM techniques have been described as both religious and non-religious as an aspect of a new religious movement, or as rooted in and as a non-religious practice for self-development.

In his 1963 book, *The Science of Being and Art of Living*, the Maharishi writes that words create waves of vibrations, and the quality of the vibration of a Mantra should correspond to the vibrational quality of the individual. The sounds used in the technique are taken from the ancient Vedic tradition have no specific meaning are are selected for their suitability for the individual. Vedic tradition and the Bija (seed,starting point, origin) Mantras are traditionally associated with particular deities and used as a form of worship.

About TM Courses:

The Transcendental Meditation technique is taught in a standardized seven-step course over six days by a certified TM teacher. The initiation begins with a short Puja (act or ritual of worship) ceremony performed by the teacher. The stated purpose of the ceremony is to show honor and gratitude to the lineage of TM Masters, or Holy Tradition that is listed in the Maharishi's translation and commentary of the Bhagavad Gita. It is regarded as putting students in the right frame of mind to receive the Mantra. The ceremony is conducted in a private room with a little while altar containing incense, camphor, rice, flowers, and a picture of Maharishi's teacher, Guru Dev. The initiate observes passively as the teacher recites a text in Sanskrit. After the ceremony the Meditators are invited to bow, receive their Mantra, and begin to Meditate.

Trataka (Candle) Meditation:

Focused gazing is a simple practice involving looking at an object, or point without blinking, then closing your eyes and visualizing it in your min's eye. This practice is commonly performed with a candle flame in a dimmed room. However, at night one could gaze at the moon or a bright star. In the daylight a flower or tree can be the focus of your gazing. Choose one point and stick with it for the practice. Performing this exercise increases the ability to focus attention and creating a sense of deep silence and rest. Trataka is also said to develop the Third Eye Chakra (Ajna) which is the seat of intuition or psychic powers. You can do this silent practice before, after, or separately from regular Meditation practice.

Steps to Practice:

Sit in a comfortable, crossed-legged position on the floor, or sitting up in a chair with feet flat on the floor.

Safely place a lighted candle 3-4 feet in front of you at eye level. (A simple measure is 1 ½ arm's length)

Take off eyeglasses (contact lenses) and adjust the distance between the candle and yourself to that you can observe a relatively clear image of the candle wick without a blur.

Gaze directly into the flame of the candle while keeping the eyes relaxed and fixing the gaze on the lighted wick. Try not to blink.

Close your eyes in case you feel eyes tired or burning.

Visualize the image of the flame at the eye brow center. If you don't see it, do not be discouraged or disappointed. This will happen with sufficient practice.

Bring your focus to that image and if the image wanders, or disappears, then bring it back by simply looking for it with your inner vision (eyes closed).

Keep the palms lightly pressed against the closed eyes.

Open eyes slowly and re-start the Meditation. Do it as often as you like for a total of 20 minutes.

At the end of your practice slowly open the eyes. Do not get immediately but move into activity slowly.

Vipassana Meditation

Vipassana means "to see things as they really are." It is one of India's most ancient techniques of Meditation and was taught in India more than 2500 years ago as a universal remedy for all illnesses. Vipassana is a way of self-transformation through self-observation by focusing on the interconnection between mind and body which can be experienced directly by focused attention to the physical sensations arising in the body. Vipassana helps us to understand that everything is impermanent and attachment to impermanent sensations, thoughts, or emotions causes instability and lack of control in our lives.

Steps to Practice:

Set Posture:

Sit in any Meditative Asana and try not to move throughout the Meditation. Review the day: Spend 2 minutes reviewing your day or any issues that you have pending in your mind. Acknowledge them and decide to put them aside for the duration of the Meditation. You can come back to them once the Meditation is over.

Beginning Prayer:

Place hands in prayer Mudra and repeat:

May I be truly happy and free from suffering. All living beings, no matter who they are, no matter what they have done to you in the past – may they all find true happiness too."

Further Instructions:

Stage 1:10 minutes   Sitting Asana Breathing –

Begin focusing on the psysical sensation of the breath coming in and out of the nostrils. All awareness should be on the nose and the upper lip during this time as you feel any sensations such as temperature, tickling, flaring of the nostrils, etc.

Stage 2: 10 minutes   Sitting Asana   Scanning –

Beginning at the top of the head scan each part of the body and only move from a section once you have felt some sensation in that area. If no sensation arises, continue to increase your attention until you can feel something. Work from the top of the head to the toes of your feet.

Stage 3: 10 minutes   Sitting Asana   Whole Body awareness –
Scan your entire body like a wave from head to toes and from toes to head. Become aware of the whole body and its vibrations and energy. In this time any physical sensations that arise you can draw your attention to and acknowledge them and then continue to scan and feel the entire body.
Stage 4: 5 Minutes   Sitting Asana   Loving Kindness –
Visualize sending out your energy and vibrations, love, and kindness to the world.

Remind Yourself:

All phenomena are impermanent. The pain in your body will pass. The tickle will dissolve. Thoughts will slide away. You are training your mind not to be reactionary to things that come into contact with your senses. You are practicing non-judgement, acceptance, and control over your actions.

Walking Meditation:

As you walk, simply attend to your senses: feel the earth beneath your feet, the movement of your body, the ever-changing balance of the body, sounds you hear, what you see, etc. This practice can help you become intimate with the body in action and for some, this creates a more observable focus than a still Meditation.

Do this Meditation for a fixed period of time as you would a sitting Meditation. It is suggested to do this technique for 10-20 minutes. You can do this by itself, or after and before a sitting Meditation period.

Select a quiet place where you can walk comfortably.

Begin by standing at one end of this walking path with your feet firmly planted on the ground.

Let your hands rest easily wherever they are comfortable. Close your eyes for a moment, center yourself, and feel your body standing on the Earth. Take a deep breath in and out.

Keep your eyes lowered as you gaze toward the ground a few steps ahead of you.

While walking, attend to the sensation of your feet. Notice the contact as they touch the ground as you feel the pressure on the bottoms of the feet, and the other natural sensation of standing.

If your attention drifts away, then notice what distracted you and then return to the feet.

Begin to walk slowly. Let yourself walk with a sense of ease and awareness. Pay attention to your body as you go from being still to movement.

With each step feel the sensations of lifting your foot and leg off of the earth. Be aware as you place each foot on the ground.

Relax and let your walking be easy and natural. Feel each step mindfully as you walk.

When you come to the end of your path then pause for a moment. Center yourself, mindfully turn around, and pause again so that you can be aware of the first step as you walk back.

97

You can experiment with the speed by walking at whatever pace keeps you most in the present.

As with any sitting Meditation the mind will wander around many, many times. As soon as you notice this acknowledge when it does and return to feel the next step. It's like training a puppy; keep bringing it back.
Whether your attention was distracted for one second, or for ten minutes, simply acknowledge where it was and come back to being in the present moment with your next step. Be kind to yourself.

When you finish this part, then experience yourself standing and notice the stillness.

Bring your attention on what is keeping you upright.

Feel your body's weight as it sinks down your legs through the soles of the feet into the earth.

Simple stand, experience yourself, and with a deep breath bring the walking Meditation session to a close.

Yantra Meditation

Gazing is a simple practice involving gazing at an object or point without blinking, then closing the yes and visualizing the image in your mind's eye. This practice is performed with a Yantra (Geometrical design) in the daylight. This practice increases the ability to focus attention and to create a sense of deep silence and rest. It is also said to develop the Ajna (Third Eye Chakra), the seat of intuition or that part associated with psychic powers. You can do this with silent practice before, after, or separately from your regular Meditation Practice.

A Yantra is a geometrical pattern made of several concentric figures (squares, circles, lotus's, triangles, Bindu (point). The Bindu at the center of the Yantra signifies unity, origin, the principle of manifestation and emanation. A yantra is the Yogic equivalent of the Buddhist Mandala (circle or essence). When these concentric figures are gradually growing away from their center (Bindu) in stages this is for human beings a symbol of the process of macrocosmic evolution.

According to Tantra, the creation of the world begins with an act of division of the opposites that are united in the Deity. From their splitting arises in an explosion of energy, the multiplicity of the world. Starting from pure unity (Shiva), the world is a continuous unfolding (energized by the power of Shakti), until a state is reached when the process must reverse and involute back to the very beginning. Multiplicity must once again become unity. Yantras are symbolic representation of this process of evolution and involution.

According to Tantra, a human being is a miniature universe. All that is found in the cosmos can be found within each individual and the same principles that apply to the universe apply in the case of the individual being. For human beings the body is considered the most perfect and powerful of all Yantras and is seen as a tool for inner awareness.

A Yantra is thus a tool making the process of evolution conscious to the adept of Tantrism. It enables the adept to retrace his steps from the outward-directed world of multiplicity to the inward focus of unity. All primal shapes of a Yantra are psychological symbols corresponding to inner states of human consciousness. Yantras are sacred symbols of the process of involution and evolution.

Steps to Practice:
Use the same steps as those used in Trataka (Candle Gazing) Meditation.

Yoga Nidra Meditation

Yoga Nidra means Psychic Sleep and is based on one of the techniques of Tantras: Nyasa means to place or establish. A process to relax the conscious mind and awaken the awareness and potential of the subconscious mind. Yoga Nidra is the borderline state of mind between sleep and wakefulness. It is a great transformative tool which prepares the mind for spiritual discipline.
According to Pierre Bonnasse, writing in *Yoga Nidra: Beyond Wakefulness, Dreams & Deep Sleep*, says,

 "As for the term "nidra," it has many meanings ... but is also designates total awareness in deep sleep, in dream state or in wakefulness; thus, it is no more than the very nature of Shiva or Vishnu. It is *That.* The term "Yoga Nidra" therefore directly refers to the union with this Presence; or rather, it refers to recognizing this Presence. For, it is not bound by a common subject-object relationship, but it refers to an intuitive holding, with no subject to hold. Hence, Yoga Nidra is both the mean's and the end leading to this."

Adi Shankaracharya, the great master of non-duality (Advaita Vedanta), writes in one of his essays:
"Through appropriate practice, done steadily when all thoughts and intentions are completely rooted out, when we are freed totally from the web of Karma, then the yogi reaches and remains in the state of Yoga Nidra. Resting in the bed of the Turiya state, higher than the other three states, always having the vision of the highest; my dear friend, enter and remain in the Nirvikalpa state, the state of Yoga Nidra."

There are three types of sleep:

Tamasic – This is a dense, without awareness sleep leaving the impression of heaviness, drowsiness in both the physical and mental states.

Rajastic – This type of sleep is troubled, agitated and filled with unclear dreams. There are too many Rajas in the heart and can cause excitability, jealousy in the waking state.

Sattvic – This state of sleeping is almost dreamless resulting in a deep contentment with more lightness, awareness, and deep clarity.

During Yoga Nidra,(Conscious sleep), it goes beyond these 3 state of ordinary awareness. The I and Me collapse, but I AM remains unaffected by sleep, dreams, or waking. Some call it the sleep of bright light.

In this state, the body is like a child being watched over by the Mother (awareness).

Steps to Practice:

Stage 1: Preparation 5-10 Minutes

Body Awareness: Description of the posture (Shavasana), letting go of the body parts by loosening the body physically and mentally, working on the body alignment.

Breath Awareness: Deep breathing three times and then allow the breath to settle down and become normal.

Mental Awareness: Awareness of the different sounds in the environment or become conscious of the sensation of the touch (Body-floor or clothes, etc.)

Stage 2: 10 Minutes

Sankalpa (Resolve): This should be a very short, positive, simple, and very clear (no ambiguity) for example: I will maintain my awareness throughout the Yoga Nidra session. This Sankalpa must be repeated three times for the Gods to hear you. Do this in the mind with faith, feeling and awareness

Stage 3: Rotation of awareness: 10-20 minutes

(In this stage, the body is essentially being put back together one piece at a time. Concentrate on each part with intense visualization and focus)

Right side: Right hand thumb, first finger, second finger, third finger, fourth finger, and then little finger. Move to palm of the right hand, back of the

100

hand, wrist, lower arm, elbow, upper arm, shoulder, arm pit, side of the chest, side of the trunk, waist, hip, thigh, back of the thigh, knee cap, back of knee, calf, shin, ankle, heel, sole, top of the foot, big toe, second toe, third toe, fourth toe, and fifth toe.

(Repeat for the left side in the same order)

Back to front side: Right buttock, left buttock, lower back, middle of back, right shoulder blade, left shoulder blade, back of neck, back of head, top of head, then forehead. Right temple, left temple, forehead (again) right eye brow, left eye brow, center of eyebrows, right eye, left eye, right cheek, left cheek, right nostril, left nostril, tip of nose, upper lip, lower lip, chin, front of neck, chest, abdomen, lower part of the abdomen.

Stage 4: Awareness/Senstion/Visualization 10-20 Minutes

Breath awareness: Simple abdominal breathing. Counting of breaths may be added Begin by counting down breaths from 108, 54, or 27 with an inhale and exhale for each breath taken. Alternate nostril breathing can also be attempted without the use of the fingers to block the breath, and instead is done consciously.
Opposite sensations: Bodily sensations of heaviness and lightness, heat and cold, sensation of fatigue and vitality, pain and pleasure, hatred and love, etc.

Visualization: Rapid objects visualization consisting of soothing images and forms. Story visualization, body organs visualization, daily activity visualization, etc.

Specific visualization: Using Chakra symbols, lotus, colors of the lotus, Yantra, etc.

Repeat Sankalpa 3 times

Stage 5: Finish 10 minutes

Externalization: Bring the awareness on the Breath, Body, external environment, and move the body slowly.

Section III

Pictorial Guide and Additional Information

Meditation Glossary

Terms	Description
Agni Tattva Tattva's	Fire Element: from the five basic
Agnisar Kriya	One of the Shatkarmas (cleansing practices) intestinal cleansing
Aham	Ego
Ahimsa Yamas of Astanga Yoga	Non-violence, non-injury. One of the
Ajapa Japa Mantra	Spontaneous repetition of Soham
Ajna Chakra	Energy center located behind the forehead, also referred to as psychic center
Akasha	Ether or space
Anahata Chakra	Energy center located in the heart region; also referred to as Pranic center
Ananda	Bliss or ecstasy
Ardha Padmasana	Half-lotus pose
Asana	Yoga position or Yoga pose, also referred to as Yogasana
Ashrama	Residential place of people living together in the Yogic tradition

Ashtanga Yoga	The eight-fold path of Yoga as outlined by Patanjali: Yama…to Samadhi
Ashwini Mudra	Practice of contracting the anal sphincter
Avidya	Ignorance
Bandha	A posture in which organs and muscles are contracted to create an energy lock in specific areas
Bhagvad Gita	A part of the famous Hindu epic Mahabharata which are teaching of Lord Krishna to his disciple Arguna at the commencement of the battle of Kurukshetra with explanation on Sannyasa Yoga, Karma Yoga, Bhakti Yoga, and Jnana Yoga.
Bhakti Yoga	The yoga of devotion
Bhastrika Pranayama	Bellows breathing technique in which the breath is forcibly drawn in and out through the nose in equal proportions like the pumping action of the bellows.
Bhramari Pranayama	Breathing practice in which a soft humming bee sound is produced during exhalation to stimulate the Ajna Chakra
Chakra	Circle or wheel referring to the energy centers lying along the confluence of the Nadis (energy channels)
Chandra	Moon
Chandra Nadi	Ida Nadi, or left channel of energy running along the spine
Chidakasha	Psychic space in front of the closed eyes just behind the forehead
Chin Mudra	Hand gesture in which the first finger is kept at the root of the thumb with the last 3 fingers are unfolded and together
Dharana	Practice of concentration; sixth of the eight fold path in Ashtanga Yoga

Dhyana	Meditation; single pointed focus of mind on either a form, thought, or sound
Dosha	Three humours of the body; see Kapha, Pitta, Vata
Ghrita Neti	Neti (nasal purification technique) performed with Ghee or Oil
Guru	Spiritually enlightened soul who can dispel darkness, ignorance, and illusion from the mind and enlighten the consciousness of a devotee, or disciple.
Hatha Yoga	Science of Yoga which purifies the whole physical body by means of Shatkarma, Asana, Pranayama, Mudra, Bandha, and concentration
Hridaya Akasha	Psychic space of the heart center
Ida Nadi	One of the main energy channels running on the left side of the spine from the Mooladhara (base) Chakra to the Ajna Chakra in the head. Also known as the Chandra Nadi
Jala Tattva	Water element
Jala Neti	A Shatkarma technique which is cleansing of nasal passages with water by alternating the flow of water in the nostrils preferably using a Neti pot.
Jalandhara Bandha	Throat lock to restrict the flow of breath through the throat done by resting the chin on the upper sternum, or chest.
Japa	Continuous chanting; or repetition of a Mantra
Jnana Mudra	The gesture of knowledge. In this hand position the index finger is bent so that its tip is joined with the tip of the thumb; the other three fingers are spread out
Jnana Yoga	The Yoga of knowledge attained through spontaneous self-analysis and investigation of abstract ideas.

Kapalbhati Pranayama	A breathing technique aimed at cleaning the frontal part of the brain. Also called skull polishing and done through rapid breaths with more force on the exhalation.
Karma Yoga	The Yoga of action which aims at supreme consciousness through action and is discussed in the Bhagavad Gita
Klesha	Affliction or tensions which according to Yoga there are 5 such afflictions present in humans from birth
Kosha	Sheath or body; realm of experience and existence
Kumbhaka	Breath retention
Kundalini Yoga	Philosophy expounding the awakening of potential energy and inherent consciousness within the human body and mind.
Manipura Chakra	The energy center in the spinal column located behind the navel corresponding to the solar plexus
Mantra	Subtle sound vibration which through repetition aims at expanding one's awareness or consciousness
Moksha	Liberation from the cycle of birth and death.
Moola Bandha	Energy lock created by the contraction of the perineum in the male and the cervix in the female
Mooladhara Chakra	Lowest energy center in the human body where the Kundalini Shakti (serpent power) resides situated in the perineal floor in men and the cervix in women.
Mudra	Literally means gesture. Mudras express and channels cosmic energy within the mind and body.

Nadi Shodhana Pranayama	Breathing technique known as alternate nostril breathing or balanced breathing. This balances the energy flow in the channels and purifies the energy channels (nadi) by balancing the flow of breath through the right and left nostrils.
Nauli	A cleansing technique (Shatkarma) involving the contraction of the rectus abdominal muscles.
Niyama	Rule. There are 5 rules described in the Ashtanga Yoga of Patanjali
Om	The universal Mantra. The cosmic vibration of the universe which represents the four state of consciousness
Padmasana	Lotus Pose. A seated Meditative posture.
Panchatatva	The five elements: Earth Water, Fire, Air, and Ether
Param	Highest, Supreme, God
Patanjali	Author of the Yoga Sutras and preacher of the eight-fold (Ashtanga) Yoga
Pingala Nadi	One of the main energy channels running on the right side of the spine from the Mooladhara (base) Chakra to the Ajna Chakra in the head by intersecting various Chakras on the way.
Prakasha	Inner light
Prakriti	Nature
Pranayama Mudra	Hand gestures adopted during Pranayama to alternate the flow of breath through the nostrils
Pranayama	Technique of breathing and breath control which regulates and enhances energy glow

Prasad	An offering usually food to and from the Guru or higher power
Pratyahara	Sense withdrawal. The first stage of concentrating on the mind during Meditation.
Prithvi Tattwa	The Earth element
Purusha	Man or pure consciousness
Raja Yoga	Yoga in which union is achieved through concentration of mind
Rechaka	Exhalation
Sahasrara Chakra	The highest energy center located at the crown of the head
Samadhi	The final stage of Ashtanga Yoga in which concentration becomes one with the object of concentration
Samskara	Impressions stored in the mind that form the basis of our beliefs, attitudes and personality.
Sankalpa	Spiritual resolve
Santosha	Contentment
Satya	Truth (one of the Yamas)
Shakti	Vital force or energy
Shambhavi Mudra	A Yoga gesture in which one focuses at the mid-eyebrow center
Shatkarma	The six Yogic techniques of purification of the body: Vis, Neti, Dhauti, Nauli, Basti, Trataka, Kapalbhati
Shishya	Disciple or student
Siddha Yoni Asana	The female counterpart of the Siddhasana Meditative posture in which the left heel presses the entrance to the vagina
Siddhasana	A Meditative seating posture in which the left heel presses the perineum

	(stimulating the Mooladhara Chakra) also called as the adept's pose or the Pose of Perfection.
Sirshasana	Inverted pose – the headstand in which the body is inverted and balanced on the crown of the head
Soham	Represents a Mantra in Meditation which literally means, I am That and is the Psychic sound with the sound So during inhalation and Ham during exhalation.
Sukhasana	A comfortable Meditative pose also called the easy pose or simply the cross-legged pose
Surya Nadi	See Pingala Nadi: The pingala is known as the right channel because it flows to the right as it leaves the *muladhara* (root) chakra and weaves in and out of the other chakras before ending at the right nostril.
Sushumna Nadi	The main energy channel in Yoga located in the center of the spinal cord through which Kundalini Shakti flows
Svadhistthana Chakra	The second Chakra in the spinal column located above the Mooladhara
Swastikasana	The auspicious pose (Meditative posture similar to Siddhasana).
Tadasana	Palm tree pose – Standing posture
Tattva	The five basic elements Fire, Air, Ether (space), Earth, Water
Trataka	One of the Purification techniques (Shatkarma) in which the gaze is focused upon an object such as a candle flame.
Uddiyana Bandha	The abdominal retraction lock where one draws in the abdomen towards the backbone after exhaling

Ujjayi Pranayama	A kind of breathing technique which produces a light sonorous sound.
Vajrasana	The Thunderbolt pose which is a kneeling posture with buttocks resting upon the heels.
Vayu Tattwa	Air element
Vedas	The four ancient texts: Riug, Yajur, Sama, Atharva. They were revealed to the sages and saints of India which explain and regulate every aspect of life from supreme reality to worldly affairs.
Vishuddhi Chakra	One of the energy centers located in the spine behind the throat and connected with the cervical plexus, tonsils, and thyroid gland
Yoga	State of union between two opposites – body and mind; individual and universal consciousness; a process of uniting the opposing forces in the body and mind in order to achieve supreme awareness and enlightenment.
Yoga Nidra	A deep relaxation technique also called Yogic Sleep in which mind and body is at complete rest, but with complete awareness.

Typical Meditation Session (Structure)

- **Duration:** 75 Minutes (Approximately)

- **Step 1 –** 3-5 Minutes –

  Have students assume an easy sitting position, eyes closed gently, with hands in the Namaskar (Anjali) Mudra with chanting for a minimum of 3 minutes led by the Instructor. Chanting creates a relationship between the student and Instructor which is a great tool for achieving a flow for the Meditation to come. Any chant, mantra, Bhajan, or prayer is good and singing can also be a part of this step.

- **Step 2 -** 10-15 minutes
  Once the opening Chant is complete, say, "Namaste," ask students to bow and then open their eyes. Students can relax as the Instructor begins to explain the Meditation they are about to be part of. Here, the instructor will

give a brief explanation demonstrating the background, precautions, and benefits. This will be brief and does not go too far into detail offering only practical information.

- **Step 3 –** 10 minutes
  This portion of the class will be devoted to stretching and warming up of the muscles in preparation for the extended period of sitting often found in most Meditations and can consist of the following:
  o Breathing: Bhramari, Ujjayi, Bhastrika
  o Yoga positions – Sun Salutations
  o Aerobic – jumping, twisting, dancing, etc

- **Step 4 –** Meditation 30 minutes

  (Note: for most Meditation session end in Shavasana as students Meditate on previous session effects) Bring their awareness back to the studio and before rising to a comfortable sitting position, have them turn on right side (if day) and left if evening) This helps in balancing the Ha and Tha.

- **Step 5 –** 3-5 minutes
  End in Chant (prayer, Mantra, Bhajan)

- **Step 6 –** 10 minutes
  Allow time once the session is ended for feedback from students. If no one offers any, then ask a few questions to encourage speaking by students.

Sample Meditation Sessions

(Note: Steps 1-4, 6, & 13-14 will be done for all Meditation Sessions. The remaining steps will be pertinent to the Meditation being performed.)

Trataka (Candle Meditation) Duration: 1 hour and 15 minutes

Step 1: (Steps 1-5 should take about 5-10 minutes)

Provide each student with a tissue for blotting of the eyes if tears should occur. Begin by having students sit in Sukasana (the easy sitting position or any other Asana which they find comfortable) with eyes gently closed, and normal breathing through the nose. Hands should be resting on the knees in Jnana/Chin Mudra, or any of the other Mudras shown in Section II, part C.

Step 2:

110

Direct students to take three, long cleansing breaths (Pura – inhalation and Rechaka – exhalation)

Step 3:

Have students bring their hands to heart (Namaskar Mudra)

Step 4:

Open the session with a Prayer, Mantra, or Bhajan (example: Om Arogym Om Alocam Om Anandam)

Step 5:

Students should now open their eyes and relax as you explain the Trataka Meditation. (Spend no more than 5 minutes) Use the information provided in the Practical portion of this manual to provide details about Trataka: focused gazing without blinking, benefits of this eye Shatkarma.

Step 6: (Stretching and Breathing Exercises should be about 5 minutes in duration)

Have students perform some simple stretching exercises. These can be Yoga stretches such as the Sun Salutation. Also, trunk twists, sitting leg stretch, neck rotations, eye movement in circles, etc.Once the stretching exercises are complete, have students perform Pranayama such as Ujjayi breath, Bhramari Breath, or Spinal Breathing. Brhamari breath is a good way to begin a Meditation session as it has a calming effect on the mind, as well as a soothing effect on the brain.

Step 7: (10 minutes)

Have students sit approximately 1 ½ arms length away from the candle flame which should be at eye level. Ask them to stare at the base of the flame without blinking for as long as possible. This may seem difficult at first, but with more practice it should become easier.

Step 8: (5 minutes)

Have students reflect/meditate within the Chidakasha (the space within the forehead and 3rd eye) with eyes closed and normal breathing. Focusing their attention in this area will engage the Ajna Chakra as they attempt to recreate the visions seen within the candle flame.

Step 9: (10 minutes)

This is round 2 where students once again gaze into the flame, but this time have them look at the center portion. There may be a haze surrounding this part and scenes may appear with a background, persons, colors, objects, etc.

Step 10: (5 minutes)

Students will close their eyes once again and focus their attention on the Chidakasha as they reflect/meditate on what has been presented to them in the flame.

Step 11: (10 minutes)

Round 3 is the final part where student once again open their eyes and gaze into the flame, however, have them place their attention at the top of the flame.

Step 12: (10 minutes)

In this final stage, have students lie in Shavasana (Corpse pose) and bring their attention to the Chidakasha. They should be reflecting/meditating on the entire experience during their meditative session.

Step 13: (5 Minutes)

In a quiet and soothing voice ask the students to return their awareness back to the room and leave their intense reflection/meditation on their Trataka experience. Direct them to begin small movements of the fingers and toes, hands and feet, arms and legs, etc. Advise them when they are ready to turn to their right side (if evening), or left (day) and have them lay their for a minute or so. Then, ask them to take an easy sitting position once more and bring hands to the Namashka Mudra (hands to heart). Close the session with a Mantra, Prayer, or Bhajan.

Step 14: 10 minutes

This final stage of the Meditation is for student feedback. Encourage them to discuss their experience. Sometimes students are hesitant to share and it may take some encouragement from you to get them to reveal what occurred during their meditation. As their teacher you may offer what
others have discussed during past Meditation sessions.

Yoga Nidra Meditation

The following information is taken from *Yoga Nidra* by Pierre Bonnasse and Vivek Bansal (who loved 20 years as a Sadhu in India and is lifelong practitioner of Yoga Nidra)

Preparation. In order to complete this stage, the proper environment is critical. Yoga Nidra relies on quiet and comfort so the room should reflect this. Students should not be disturbed by outside noises (if possible) and the room temperature should not be too hot or cold where it affects the student.

Step 1-4: **Opening Steps** 5 minutes *(Steps 1-4 should follow the same structure as outlined in the previous session)*

Step 5: **Explanation of the Yoga Nidra Meditation** 5 minutes

Students should now open their eyes and relax as you explain the Yoga Nidra Meditation. Use the information provided in the Practical portion of this manual to provide details about Yoga Nidra, also known as Psychic Sleep. Inform students they will need to decide on a Sankalpa (resolve) which will be a short, positive, simple, and clear statement of some area they wish to effect change in their lives.

Relaxation: 5 minutes

In order to be more receptive, the body should be relaxed and free of tensions. The following exercises are suited for this:

Stiffness of the corpse exercise: In Shavasana, bring the arms close to the body, breathe in and then hold the breath. Contract the body while tightening the arms against the sides. Let go with exhalation. Pay close attention to as the body relaxes and becomes unmoving.

Wave exercise: Intensifies relaxation and sensitivity. Inhale and feel the breath's touch rising in front of the body beginning at the bottoms of the feet to the top of the head and then behind the body with exhalation beginning at the back of the head, back, and down the legs to the feet. Have students imagine this as a wave of relaxation with each inhalation across the front and down the back with exhalation. This becomes like a wave on the ocean of the body.

Sankalpa: 5 minutes

With intense relaxation comes the awakening of intuition. Participants should create a Sankalpa (resolve) using positive thoughts to create the reality of the resolve. Have students inhale and repeat this Sankalpa 3 times during Antah Kumbhaka (breath held after inhalation). This can be focused in the Chidakasha (3rd eye space) or in the Anahata (heart chakra space). The Sankalpa must be repeated 3 times in order for the gods to hear.

Step 8: **Rotation of Consciousness** 10 minutes

(look in the Practical section, Yoga Nidra Meditation for the parts of the body and their location as well as the order for them to be focused on).

Step 9: **Breath Awareness** 5 minutes

Simple abdominal breathing. Counting of breaths may be added and is done by counting down breaths from 108, 54, or 27 with an inhale and exhale for each breath taken. Alternate nostril breathing can also be attempted without the use of the fingers to block the breath, and instead is done consciously.

Step 10: **Opposite Sensations**: 5 minutes

Opposite sensations: Bodily sensations of heaviness and lightness, heat and cold, sensation of fatigue and vitality, pain and pleasure, hatred and love, etc.

113

Step 11: **Visualization** 5 minutes

Visualization: Rapid objects visualization consisting of soothing images and forms. Story visualization, body organs visualization, daily activity visualization, etc. Specific visualization: Using Chakra symbols, lotus, colors of the lotus, Yantra, etc.

Step 12: **Sankalpa** 5 minutes

Have students recall the Sankalpa used in the beginning of the Yoga Nidra Meditation. Their thoughts should be focused as they bring their attention once more to the intention they had set and as done previously during Antah Kumbhaka, repeat the Sankalpa three times.

Steps 13-14 **Completion of Meditation** 15 minutes (See the previous meditation for completing these last portions of the Yoga Nidra Meditation.

Nada Yoga Meditation

(Note: Steps 1-4, 6, & 13-14 will be done for all Meditation Sessions. The remaining steps will be pertinent to the Meditation being performed. These steps are outlined in the first sample meditation.)

Step 1-4: Opening Steps 5 minutes *(Steps 1-4 should follow the same structure as outlined in the previous session)*

Step 5: **Explanation of the Nada Yoga Meditation. (See page 70).**

Step 7:Perform the following while standing using the sounds which make up OM. Use either hand for placement on the body Chakra and the other in Chin Mudra

A (aahhh) – This syllable represents the origin of all sound, connecting us to our individual selves, or egos. This resonance should come from the back of the throat where the tongue finds its root in our physical being.

U (oooh) – This syllable represents the energy of the mind and the universe. This vibration invokes balance and clarity as it passes from the back of the tongue toward the lips.

M (mmmm) – This syllable invokes the sensation of oneness between the corporal body and the universe. Practitioners close their lips around the sound to experience the vibration throughout their head and body
Step 8:
A – 7 times with hand on the Navel (Manipura)
Step 9:
U – 7 times with hand on the Heart (Anaahata)
Step 10:

M – 7 times with hand on the Throat (Vishuddha)

Step 11:

Assume an easy sitting position with hands in Chin Mudra using ear plugs and eyes closed. Begin Bhramari Pranayama (Humming Bee Breath) for 10 minutes. Sit in silence and Meditate on the vibrations created by Bhramari Pranayama for 10 minutes.

Listen to music for 10 minutes. (Note: the music selected should contain different sounds. An excellent choice would be: Zolfeggio Frequencies due to its variant and soothing nature. Note: Be sure to have the volume high in order for participants to hear the music. At the end of the allocated time period, and with ear plugs still in place Meditate on the sounds heard during this music for 10 minutes.

Step 12

Lie down in Shavasana, remove the ear plugs, and keep the eyes closed. Meditate on all internal sounds for 10 minutes.

Steps 13 & 14

See the first sample meditation and repeat these steps here.

OVER VIEW OF PRACTICES

KAPALBHATI	PANCH TATTVA	DHYAN MUDRA	ASHWANI MUDRA
UJJAYI	BHRUMADHYA	BHAIRAV MUDRA	NASIKAGRA MUDRA
ANULOM VILOM	PURNA NIMESH	CHIN MUDRA	VIPRIT KARANI MUDRA
BHASTRIKA	ARDH NIMESH	GYAN MUDRA	TRI BANDHA
BHRAMARI	SAMA DRISHTI	VISHNU MUDRA	SHANMUKHI MUDRA
PRANAYAMAMUDRA	NASIKAGRA DRISHTI	KHECHARI MUDRA	MEDITATION POSTURE

P 23

116

MANTRA 1

Om Puurnna-madah Puurnna-midam
Puurnna-at Purnna-mud-acyate
Puurnna-shya Puurnna-maa-daaya
Puurnna-mevaa-vashis-syate

Om Shaantih Shaantih Shaantih

Om, That is Full, This also is Full, From Fullness comes that Fullness, Taking Fullness
from Fullness, Fullness Indeed Remains. Om Peace, Peace, Peace.

MANTRA 2

Gurur-brahmaa gurur-vishnur guruedevo mahe-shwarah;
Guruh saakshaat param brahma tasmai shree gurave namah.
Guru is the creator (Brahma); Guru is the preserver (Vishnu);
Guru is the destroyer (Maheshvara); Guru is verily the
Supreme Absolute. To that Guru we prostrate.

MANTRA 3

Om Bhuur-Bhuvah Svah
Tatsa-vitur-Varen-nyam I
Bhargo Devasya Dhiimahi
Dhiyo Yo Nah Praco-dayaat I I

Meaning: Om, that (Divine Illumination) which pervades the Bhu Loka (Physical
Plane), Bhuvar Loka (Antariksha Loka or the Astral Plane) and Suvar Loka (Swarga
Loka or the Celestial Plane), That Savitr (Divine Illumination) which is the Most
Adorable, On that Divine Radiance we Meditate, May that Enlighten Our Intellect and
Awaken our Spiritual Wisdom.

MANTRA 4

Hare Ram Hare Ram, Ram Ram Hare Hare,
Hare Krishna Hare Krishna, Krishna Krishna Hare Hare
MANTRA 5

lokäl.n samastäh sukhino bhavantu
(low-kaah,-ha. suh,,muh-staah'-ha soo.khee.no bhuh vun too)

lokah: location, realm, -all universes existing now
samastah: all beings sharing that same location
sukhino: centered in happiness and joy, free from suffering;
bhav: the divine mood or state of unified existence; antu: may it be so, it must be
so

PRAYER 1

Asato maa sad-gamaya
Tamaso maa jyotir-gamaya
Mrityor-ma-amritam gamaya
0m shaantib shaantih shaantih
Lead us from Un-real to real, from
Darkness to Light, from Death to
Immortality. 0m peace, peace, peace

PRAYER 2

Sarve bhavantu sukhinah,
Sarve santu niramayah,
Sarve bhadrani pashyantu,
Ma kaschit dukha bhag-bhavet
Let all be happy. Let all be free from disease.
Let all see the Truth.
May no one experience suffering.

PRAYER 3

0m Aa-rogyam, 0m Aa-lokam, 0m
Aa-nandam, 0m Shanti x3

BHA.JAN 1

0m Namo Narayana, Narayana, Narayana

BHAJAN 2

Sri Mann Narayan Narayan Hari Hari,
Bhaj mann Narayan Narayan Hari Hari

BHAJAN 3

Tu-hi Bhaj re manaa
Tu-hi Japa re manaa
0m Shri Ram Jai Ram Japa re manaa

BHAJAN 4

Sita Ram, Sita Ram, Sita Ram say
As Lord keeps you so you stay,
May world be good or be bad,
Think it Lord's will don't be sad,
May be sad or may be gay,
Moods are fleeting, sing and pray,
Sing and pray, night and day,
Without saying Sita Ram don't pass away.

Wonders of 5 (Panch)

An Overview

Tattva	Tanmatra	Senses	Organs of Action	Klesha	Prana	Kosha
Akash (space)	Sound	Ear	Mouth	Avidya (Ignorance)	Udana	Annamaya Kosha (food sheath)
Vayu (air)	Touch	Skin	Hands	Asmita (Egoism)	Prana	Pranamaya Kosha (air sheath)
Agni (fire)	Sight	Eyes	Feet	Raga (Cravings)	Samana	Manomaya Kosha (mind sheath)
Jala (water)	Taste	Tongue	Genital	Dvesha (Aversions)	Apana	Vunanamaya Kosha (wisdom sheath)
Prithvi (earth)	Smell	Nose	Anus	Abhinibhesha (Clinging to life)	Vyana	Anandamaya Kosha (bliss sheath

The Eight Limbs of Yoga

Union, absorption	SAMADHI				
Meditation	DHYANA				
Focus	DHARANA				
Sense withdrawal	PRATYAHARA				
Breath	PRANAYAMA				
Postures	ASANA				
	NIYAMAS				
Personal conduct	Saucha (purity)	Satosha (content)	Svadhyaya (self-study)	Tapas (discipline)	Ishvara-pranidhana (surrender)
	YAMAS				
Moral code	Ahimsa (non-violence)	Satya (non-lying)	Asteya (non-stealing)	Brahmacharya (non-waste of vital energies)	Aparigraha (non-greed)

SEVEN CHAKRA MEDITATION

Chakra	1st Chakra	2nd Chakra	3rd Chakra	4th Chakra	5th Chakra	6th Chakra	7th Chakra
Chakra Name	Root Chakra	Sacral Chakra	Solar Chakra	Heart Chakra	Throat Chakra	Third Eye Chakra	Crown Chakra
Sanskrit Name	Muldhara Chakra	Svadhishthana Chakra	Manipura Chakra	Anahata Chakra	Vishuddha Chakra	Ajna Chakra	Sahasrara Chakra
Location	Base of Spine	Below the Navel	Navel	Center of Chest	Throat	Eyebrow centre	Top of Head
Color	Red	Orange	Yellow	Green	Blue	Indigo	Violet
Element	Earth	water	fire	air	space	beyond	beyond
	I am	I feel	I do	I love	I speak	I see	I under stand
Balanced Attributes	Stability	Sexuality	Self-Esteem	Self-Love	Communi-cation	Intuition	Divine Connection
Imbalanced Attributes	Scattered Energies	Sexual Dysfunction	Low Self Esteem	Depression	Shy Withdrawn	Lack of Direction	Cynicism
Location of Physical Issues	Legs Feet	Reproductive Organs	Intestines Stomach	Heart Circulatory System	Throat Lungs Thyroid	Eyes Ears	Brain
Nature Therapy	Gardening Hiking and Earth Sitting	Sexual Expression and Creative Expression	Sunshine Sunbathing and Practicing Healthy Boundaries	Self-Time and Pampering Yourself	Singing Chanting Meaningful Discussions	Dreaming of Possibilities	Meditation Cloud Watching Star Gazing

121

THE BHAGAVAD GITA SAAR (SUMMARY)

Why do you worry without cause?
Whom do you fear without reason?
Who can kill you? The soul is neither born, nor does it die.

Whatever happened, happened for the good;
whatever is happening, is happening for the good;
whatever will happen, will also happen for the good only.

You need not have any regrets for the past.
You need not worry for the future. The present is happening...
What did you lose that you cry about?
What did you bring with you, which you think you have lost?

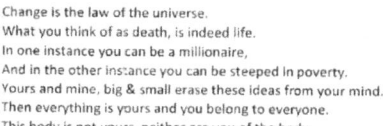

Bhagavad Gita

What did you produce, which you think got destroyed?
You did not bring anything, whatever you have, you received from here.
Whatever you have given, you have given only here.
Whatever you took, you took from God. Whatever you gave, you gave to Him.
You came empty handed, you will leave empty handed.

What is yours today, belonged to someone else yesterday,
And will belong to someone else the day after tomorrow.
You are mistakenly enjoying the thought that this is yours.
It is this false happiness that is the cause of your sorrows.

Change is the law of the universe.
What you think of as death, is indeed life.
In one instance you can be a millionaire,
And in the other instance you can be steeped in poverty.
Yours and mine, big & small erase these ideas from your mind.
Then everything is yours and you belong to everyone.
This body is not yours, neither are you of the body.
The body is made of fire, water, air, earth and ether, and will disappear into these elements.
But the soul is permanent - so who are you?

Dedicate your being to God. He is the one to be ultimately relied upon.
Those who know of his support are forever free from fear, worry and sorrow.
Whatever you do, do it as a dedication to God.
This will bring you the tremendous experience of joy and life-freedom forever.

ENERGY POINTS

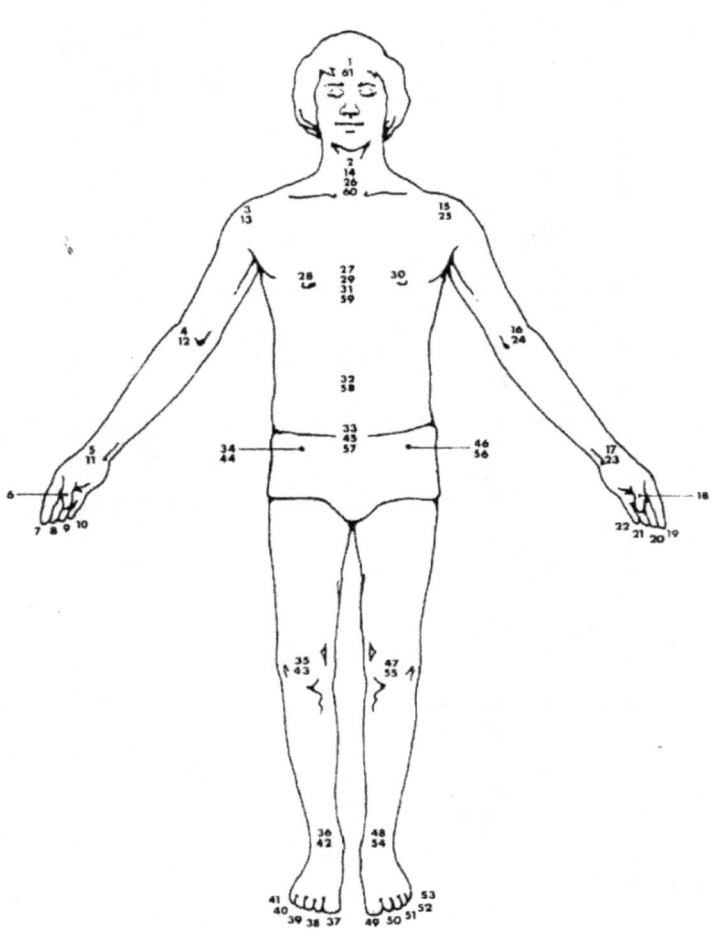

ρ 24

123

Yantra Geometric Figures

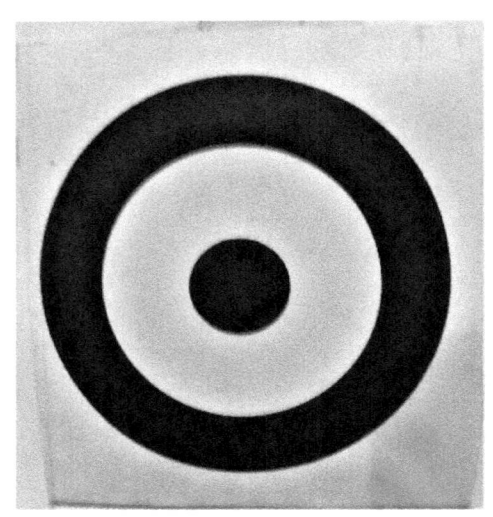

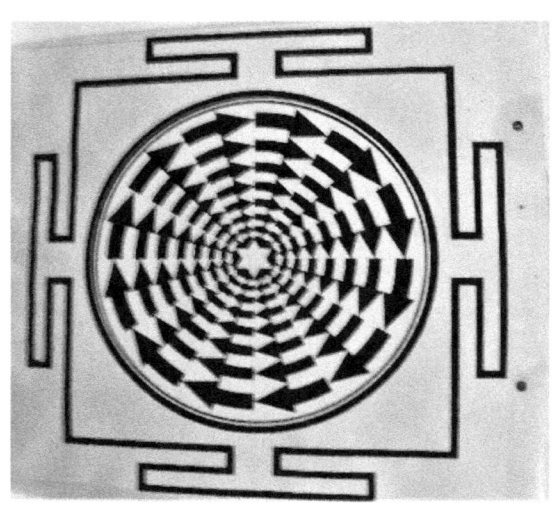